FIFTH EDITION

HTML5
Pocket Reference

Jennifer Niederst Robbins

Beijing · Cambridge · Farnham · Köln · Sebastopol · Tokyo

HTML5 Pocket Reference, Fifth Edition
by Jennifer Niederst Robbins

Copyright © 2013 Littlechair, Inc. All rights reserved.
Printed in the United States of America.

Published by O'Reilly Media, Inc., 1005 Gravenstein Highway North, Sebastopol, CA 95472.

O'Reilly books may be purchased for educational, business, or sales promotional use. Online editions are also available for most titles (*http://my.safari booksonline.com*). For more information, contact our corporate/institutional sales department: 800-998-9938 or *corporate@oreilly.com*.

Editors: Simon St. Laurent and Meghan Blanchette
Production Editor: Kristen Borg
Proofreader: Amanda Kersey
Indexer: Lucie Haskins
Cover Designer: Karen Montgomery
Interior Designer: David Futato

January 2000:	First Edition.
January 2002:	Second Edition.
May 2006:	Third Edition.
December 2009:	Fourth Edition.
August 2013:	Fifth Edition.

Revision History for the Fifth Edition:

2013-07-19	First release
2013-08-16	Second release
2013-10-25	Third release

See *http://oreilly.com/catalog/errata.csp?isbn=9781449363352* for release details.

ISBN: 978-1-449-36335-2

[LSI]

1382371169

Contents

HTML5 Pocket Reference

HTML (*HyperText Markup Language*) is the markup language used to turn text documents into web pages and applications. The fundamental purpose of HTML as a markup language is to provide a *semantic* description (the meaning) of the content and establish a document *structure* (a hierarchy of elements).

This pocket reference provides a concise yet thorough listing of the elements and attributes specified in the HTML5 Candidate Recommendation maintained by the World Wide Web Consortium (W3C) dated December 17, 2012, the HTML 5.1 Editor's Draft dated June 15, 2013, and the "living" HTML specification maintained by the Web Hypertext Application Technology Working Group (WHATWG) as of June 15, 2013.

Elements and attributes from the HTML 4.01 Specification that were made obsolete in HTML5 have been omitted from this edition. The elements and attributes contained in this book may be used in HTML 4.01, XHTML 1.0, or XHTML 1.1 documents, unless they are explicitly marked "Not in HTML 4.01," in which case they will cause the document to be invalid.

HTML5 documents can be written in XHTML syntax (formally known as the "XML Serialization of HTML5"), so whenever applicable, special considerations for XHTML will be noted. See Appendix B at the end of this reference for details on XHTML syntax requirements.

This book is organized into the following sections:

- HTML5 Overview
- HTML5 Global Attributes
- Alphabetical List of Elements
- Elements Organized by Function
- Appendix A, *Character Entities*
- Appendix B, *XHTML Syntax Overview*

HTML5 Overview

HTML5 offers new features (elements, attributes, event handlers, and APIs) for easier web application development and more sophisticated form handling.

The HTML5 specification is based on HTML 4.01 Strict, but unlike previous HTML Recommendations, HTML5 does not use a Document Type Definition (DTD). Instead, it uses the Document Object Model (DOM, the "tree" formed by a document's structure) as its basis rather than a particular set of syntax rules. It also differs from previous recommendations in that it includes detailed instructions for how browsers should handle malformed and legacy markup.

W3C and WHATWG

There are two organizations maintaining slightly different HTML specifications as of this writing.

HTML5 was originally written by the Web Hypertext Application Technology Working Group (WHATWG). In 2003, members of Apple, Mozilla, and Opera formed the WHATWG to further the development of HTML in a way that was consistent with real-world authoring practices and browser behavior. Their initial documents, Web Applications 1.0 and Web Forms 1.0, were rolled together into HTML5, which is still in development under the guidance of WHATWG editor, Ian Hickson. They eventually dropped the version number and now maintain "living" (unnumbered) HTML specification at *whatwg.org*.

In 2006, the World Wide Web Consortium (W3C) formed its own HTML5 Working Group based on the work by the WHATWG. In 2009, it discontinued its work on XHTML 2.0 in order to focus on the development of HTML5. The W3C maintains a "snapshot" (numbered) version of HTML5 (*www.w3.org/TR/html5/*), which is expected to reach Recommendation status in 2014. HTML5.1 is also in development and is scheduled to become a Recommendation in 2016. Nightly builds of the HTML5.1 Editor's Draft are available at *www.w3.org/html/wg/drafts/html/master/*.

The differences between the W3C and HTML5 Candidate Recommendation and the WHATWG versions are fairly minor. The WHATWG and HTML5.1 spec change frequently, but the differences as of this writing include:

WHATWG only

> ping attribute on a and area elements
> srcset attribute on img element

WHATWG and W3C HTML5.1 only

> data element
> menuitem element
> dialog element
> main element
> inert global attribute
> itemid, itemprop, itemref, itemscope, and itemtype global
>> attributes
> onclose and onsort global event handlers
> download attribute on a and area elements
> sortable attribute on table element
> sorted attribute on th element

W3C HTML5 only

> command element (replaced by menuitem)
> media attribute on a element
> pubdate attribute on time element

New Semantic Elements in HTML5

HTML5 includes new semantic elements for marking up page content. Details for each of these elements are provided in the section "Alphabetical List of Elements" on page 14:

article	figcaption	output
aside	figure	progress
audio	footer	rp
bdi	header	rt
canvas	hgroup*	ruby
command*	keygen	section
data**	main**	source
datalist	mark	time
details	menuitem**	track
dialog**	meter	video
embed	nav	wbr

* Removed from HTML5.1

** WHATWG and HTML5.1 only

New input types

HTML5 introduces the following new input control types (indicated as values for the type attribute for the input element): color, date, datetime, datetime-local, email, month, number, range, search, tel, time, url, and week.

Obsolete HTML 4.01 elements

The following HTML 4.01 elements were made obsolete in HTML5 because they were presentational, confusing, or poorly supported: acronym, applet, basefont, big, center, dir, frame, frameset, font, isindex, noframes, strike, and tt.

HTML5 APIs

With a growing demand for interactive content on web pages, HTML5 introduces many APIs (*Application Programming Interfaces*) for the creation of web applications. APIs standardize tasks that traditionally required proprietary plug-ins or custom programming. Some have markup components such as audio, video, and canvas; others only use JavaScript and/or server-side components.

The following APIs are part of the W3C HTML5 specification:

- **Media API**, for playback of video and audio files with multimedia synchronization and timed subtitles, used with the new video and audio elements (*bit.ly/17EC8HT* and *bit.ly/13xEOBr*)
- **TextTrack**, for adding timed subtitles and captions for video and audio elements (*bit.ly/16ZQm6S*)
- **Session History API**, for exposing the browser history (*bit.ly/12iDo0Q*)
- **Offline Web Applications API**, which allows web resources to be used while offline (*bit.ly/108K1mp*)
- **Editing API**, including a new global contenteditable attribute (*bit.ly/11Tw0Tv*)
- **Drag and Drop API**, including the new draggable attribute (*bit.ly/18sdPhs*)

Other HTML5-related APIs have separate specifications, including:

- **Canvas API** for two-dimensional drawing in conjunction with the new canvas element (*bit.ly/17ftf5F*)

- **Web Storage API** allows data to be stored in the browser's cache so an app can use it later (*bit.ly/168vZjW*)

- **Geolocation API** lets users share longitude and latitude information for so they are accessible to scripts in web applications (*bit.ly/168w5rQ*)

- **Web Workers API** that allows scripts to run in the background to improve performance (*bit.ly/17ECwWI*)

- **Web Sockets API** that maintains an open connection between the client and the server so data can pass between them in real time. This may be useful for multi-player games, chat, and live data streams (*bit.ly/13UfWUK*).

- **File API** gives access to files uploaded from a form input. It enables previews of the uploaded file to be shown and enables drag-and-drop uploading (*bit.ly/11sTkro*).

This is only a handful of the dozens of APIs in development. The following resources provide thorough lists of available APIs and other web technologies in an easy-to-use manner:

- *The Web Platform: Browser Technologies*, maintained by Mike Smith of the W3C (*platform.html5.org*)

- *HTML5 Landscape Overview*, by Erik Wilde (*dret.type-pad.com/dretblog/html5-api-overview.html*)

- *Web Platform Docs* (*docs.webplatform.org/wiki/apis*)

HTML5 Document Structure

HTML5 has only one version and does not reference a DTD, but HTML5 documents still require a simplified DOCTYPE declaration to trigger standards mode rendering in browsers. The following is the minimum recommended structure of a basic HTML5 document:

```
<!DOCTYPE html>
<html>
  <head>
    <title>Document Title</title>
  </head>
  <body>
      Content of document . . .
  </body>
</html>
```

HTML5 documents written in XML syntax do not require a DOCTYPE but may include an XML declaration. They should also be served as the MIME type `application/xhtml+xml` or `application/xml`. The following is a simple HTML5 document written in the XML syntax:

```
<?xml version="1.0" encoding="UTF-8"?>
<html xmlns="http://www.w3.org/1999/xhtml">
  <head>
    <title>Document Title</title>
  </head>
  <body>
      Content of document . . .
  </body>
</html>
```

HTML5 Browser Support

Most of the new HTML5 semantic elements and attributes are supported by contemporary desktop and mobile browsers (Chrome, Safari, Opera, Firefox, and Internet Explorer 9+). For browsers that do not support new elements and APIs, there is usually a JavaScript *polyfill* (patch) that simulates support. For a thorough list of existing polyfills, see Modernizr's collection at *www.github.com/Modernizr/Modernizr/wiki/HTML5-Cross-Browser-Polyfills*.

One example of a simple polyfill is the "HTML5 Shiv" script created by Remy Sharp. To make older browsers such as Internet Explorer 8 and earlier recognize new HTML5 elements (thus making them accessible to styles and scripts), you could write JavaScript to create each element in DOM one at a time.

For example, this command creates a `section` element:

```
document.createElement("section");
```

The HTML5 Shiv script, created by Remy Sharp, creates all of the new elements for you at once. To use it, simply point to the Google-hosted script shown here:

```
<!--[if lt IE 9]>
<script src="http://html5shiv.googlecode.com/svn/trunk/
html5-els.js"></script>
<![endif]-->
```

The following resources are useful for tracking HTML5 real-world support and use:

"When Can I Use…" (http://caniuse.com)
> A comparison of browser support for HTML5, CSS3, and other web technologies maintained by Alexis Deveria.

HTML5 Please (http://html5please.com)
> Recommends which HTML5 and CSS3 features are ready to use and which fallback to use when appropriate.

Wikipedia "Comparison of Layout Engines (HTML5)" (http://en.wikipedia.org/wiki/Comparison_of_layout_engines_(HTML_5))
> Charts show HTML5 support by the major browser layout engines.

HTML5 Readiness (http://html5readiness.com/)
> An interesting visualization of growing support for HTML5 and CSS3 from 2008 to present.

Validating HTML5 Documents

You can check to see if your HTML5 document is valid using the online validator at *validator.w3.org* (HTML5 support is in beta as of this writing) or *html5.validator.nu*.

HTML5 Global Attributes

A number of attributes are shared by all elements in HTML5 and are referred to collectively as the *Global Attributes*:

accesskey="*character*"
> Assigns an access key (shortcut key command) that activates or focuses the element. The value is a single character. Users may access the element by hitting Alt-<*key*> (PC) or Ctrl-<*key*> (Mac).

class="*text string*"
> Assigns one or more classification names to the element.

contenteditable="true|false"
> **Not in HTML 4.01**. Indicates the user can edit the element. This attribute is already well supported in current browser versions.

contextmenu="*id of menu element*"
> **Not in HTML 4.01**. Specifies a context menu that applies to the element. The context menu must be requested by the user, for example, by a right-click.

dir="ltr|rtl|auto"
> Specifies the direction of the element. ltr indicates left to right; rtl indicates right to left; and auto indicates that direction should be determined programmatically.

draggable="true|false"
> **Not in HTML 4.01**. Indicates the element is draggable, meaning it can be moved by clicking and holding on it, and then moving it to a new position in the window.

dropzone="copy|move|link|string:*text string type*|file:*file type*"
> **Not in HTML 4.01**. Indicates what happens when a data is dragged onto the element and what kind of data to accept. copy results in a copy of the dragged data; move moves the data to a new location; and link results in a link to the original data. Including string:text/plain allows it to accept any text string. The file: attribute indicates what type of file is accepted (e.g., file:image/png). Both the

action and accepted data may be provided, for example, `dropzone="copy string:text/plain"`.

hidden (hidden="hidden" *in XHTML)*

Not in HTML 4.01. Prevents the element and its descendants from being rendered in the user agent (browser). Any scripts or form controls in hidden sections will still execute, but they will not be presented to the user.

id="*text string*"

Assigns a unique identifying name to the element.

inert (inert="inert" *in XHTML)*

WHATWG & HTML5.1 only. Indicates that the element should be made inert, which means it cannot be selected, searched, or targeted by user interactions.

itemid="*text*"

WHATWG & HTML5.1 only. Part of the microdata system for embedding machine-readable data, the `itemid` attribute indicates a globally recognized identifier (such as an ISBN for a book). It is used in conjunction with `itemtype` in the same element containing `itemscope`.

itemprop="*text*"

WHATWG & HTML5.1 only. Part of the microdata system for embedding machine-readable data, the `item prop` attribute provides the name of the property. The content of the element provides its value. The value may also be a URL provided by the `href` attribute in `a` elements or the `src` attribute in `img`.

itemref="*space-separated list of IDs*"

WHATWG & HTML5.1 only. Part of the microdata system for embedding machine-readable data, the `item ref` attribute specifies a list of elements (by ID values) on the current page to be included in an *item*. The `itemref` attribute must be used in the same element as the `item scope` attribute that established the item.

`itemscope`

WHATWG & HTML5.1 only. Part of the microdata system for embedding machine-readable data, `itemscope` creates a new *item*, a group of properties (name/value pairs).

`itemtype="URL or reversed DNS label"`

WHATWG & HTML5.1 only. Part of the microdata system for embedding machine-readable data, the `item type` attribute indicates a standardized item type indicated by a URL (e.g., *http://vocab.example.net/book*) or a reversed DNS label (e.g., com.example.person). The `item type` attribute is used in the same element containing the `itemscope` attribute.

`lang`

Specifies the language for the element by its language code.

`xml:lang`

XHTML only. Specifies language for elements in XHTML documents.

`spellcheck="true|false"`

Not in HTML 4.01. Indicates the element is to have its spelling and grammar checked.

`style="CSS styles"`

Associates style information with an element.

`tabindex="number"`

Specifies the position of the current element in the tabbing order for the current document. The value must be between 0 and 32,767. It is used for tabbing through the links on a page (or fields in a form).

`title="text string"`

Provides a title or advisory information about the element.

`translate="yes|no"`

Not in HTML 4.01. Indicates whether the element's text content and attribute values should be translated when the document is localized. `yes` is the default; `no` leaves the element content unchanged.

The following attributes are not included in the list of Global Attributes but are permitted in HTML5 documents:

`aria-*="text string or number"`
> **Not in HTML 4.01**. Allows any of the WAI-ARIA states and properties for improving accessibility to be applied to an element, for example, `aria-hidden="true"`. The value of the attribute varies with the property. See *www.w3.org/TR/wai-aria/states_and_properties* for information on supported of states and properties.

`data-*="text string or numerical data"`
> **Not in HTML 4.01**. Enables authors to create custom data-related attributes, for example, `data-length`, `data-duration`, `data-speed`, etc., so that nonvisible data can be embedded and used by a custom application or scripts.

`role="standardized WAI-ARIA role"`
> **Not in HTML 4.01**. Assigns one of the standardized WAI-ARIA roles to an element to make its purpose clearer to users with disabilities. The landmark roles (`application`, `banner`, `complementary`, `contentinfo`, `form`, `main`, `navigation`, and `search`) play an important role in navigation on assistive devices. See *www.w3.org/TR/wai-aria/roles#role_definitions* for a complete list of allowable role values.

HTML5 Event Handlers

Unless otherwise specified, the following event handler content attributes may be specified on any HTML element:

onabort	ondragleave	onload*	onratechange
onblur*	ondragover	onloadeddata	onreset
oncancel	ondragstart	onloadedmetadata	onscroll
oncanplay	ondrop	onloadstart	onseeked
oncanplaythrough	ondurationchange	onmousedown	onseeking
onchange	onemptied	onmousemove	onselect
onclick	onended	onmouseout	onshow
onclose**	onerror*	onmouseover	onsort**
oncontextmenu	onfocus*	onmouseup	onstalled
oncuechange	oninput	onmousewheel	onsubmit
ondblclick	oninvalid	onpause	onsuspend
ondrag	onkeydown	onplay	ontimeupdate
ondragend	onkeypress	onplaying	onvolumechange
ondragenter	onkeyup	onprogress	onwaiting

NOTE

onblur, onerror, onfocus, and onload behave slightly differently when applied to the body element because the body element shares these event handlers with its parent window.

* Event handler for Window object when used with the body element.

** WHATWG and HTML5.1 only. Not in HTML5 Candidate Recommendation.

Alphabetical List of Elements

This section contains a list of all elements and attributes in HTML and the living HTML document at WHATWG. Readers are advised to watch for these labels on elements and attributes:

Required

> Attributes marked as **Required** must be included in the element for the markup to be valid.

W3C HTML5 only

> Elements and attributes marked **W3C HTML5 only** appear only in the W3C HTML5 Candidate Recommendation and do not appear in the HTML5.1 Editor's Draft or WHATWG.

WHATWG only

> Elements and attributes marked **WHATWG only** appear only in the living HTML specification maintained by the WHATWG and are not part of the W3C Recommendation.

Not in HTML 4.01

> Elements and attributes marked **Not in HTML 4.01** are new in HTML5 and will cause documents using the HTML 4.01, XHTML1.0, and XHTML 1.1 DOCTYPEs to be invalid.

XHTML only

> Attributes marked **XHTML only** apply only to documents written in XHTML (XML) syntax.

---

a

`<a> . . . </a>`

Defines an *anchor* that can be used as a hypertext link or a named fragment within the document. When the href attribute is set to a valid URI, the anchor is a hypertext link to a web page, page fragment, or another resource. The id attribute labels an anchor and

---

allows it to serve as the destination point of a link. An a element may have both `href` and `id` attributes. The `href` attribute may be omitted to use an a element as a "placeholder link."

HTML5 permits flow content (block elements) within a elements. There must be no interactive content (a, `audio` with controls, `button`, `details`, `embed`, `iframe`, `img` with `usemap`, `input`, `keygen`, `label`, `object` with `usemap`, `select`, `textarea`, and `video` with controls) contained in an a element.

Usage

Categories:
Flow content, phrasing content, interactive content, palpable content

Permitted contexts:
Where phrasing content is expected

Permitted content:
Transparent, but may not contain other interactive elements

Start/end tags:
Required/Required

Attributes

HTML5 Global Attributes

`download="file name"`
WHATWG and HTML5.1 only. Indicates the link is used for downloading a resource. The value is the name the resource file should be given on the local file system once it is downloaded.

`href="URI"`
Specifies the location of the destination document or web resource (such as an image, audio, PDF, or other media file).

`hreflang="language code"`
Specifies the base language of the target document.

```
media="all|aural|braille|handheld|print|projection|screen|
tty|tv"
```
> **Not in HTML 4.01. HTML5 only**. Describes the media for
> which the target document was designed. The default is all.
> This attribute has been removed in HTML5.1 and
> WHATWG.

```
ping="URLs"
```
> **WHATWG only**. Specifies a list of URLs that must be con-
> tacted when the link is followed, and is useful for user tracking.

```
rel="link type keyword"
```
> Describes one or more relationships from the current source
> document to the linked document. The link relationship types
> specified for a are alternate, author, bookmark, help, license,
> next, nofollow, noreferrer, prefetch, prev, search, and tag.

```
target="text"
```
> Specifies the name of the window or iframe in which the target
> document should be displayed.

```
type="MIME type"
```
> Specifies the media or content type (MIME type) of the linked
> content—for example, text/html.

Examples

To a local file:

```
<a href="filename.html"> . . . </a>
```

To an external file:

```
<a href="http://server/path/file.html"> . . . </a>
```

To send an email message (browser may trigger the user's mail program to open a new message):

```
<a href="mailto:username@domain"> . . . </a>
```

To a telephone number (mobile phone browsers may present an
alert box allowing the user to call the linked number):

```
<a href="tel:+15085551212"> . . . </a>
```

To a file on an FTP server:

```
<a href="ftp://server/path/filename"> . . . </a>
```

Creating a named anchor in HTML:

```
<a id="fragment"> . . . </a>
```

Linking to a named anchor:

```
<a href="http://server/path/file.html#fragment"> . . .</a>
```

Linking to a named anchor in the current file:

```
<a href="#fragment"> . . . </a>
```

---

abbr

```
<abbr> . . . </abbr>
```

Identifies the enclosed text as an abbreviation or acronym. The full description for it may be provided with the `title` attribute.

Usage

Categories:
Flow content, phrasing content, palpable content

Permitted contexts:
Where phrasing content is expected

Permitted content:
Phrasing content

Start/end tags:
Required/Required

Attributes

HTML5 Global Attributes

title="*text*"
When used with the `abbr` element, the `title` attribute provides the full expression for the abbreviation or acronym. This may be useful for nonvisual browsers, speech synthesizers, translation systems, and search engines.

Example

```
<abbr title="Massachusetts">Mass.</abbr>
```

```
<abbr title="World Wide Web">WWW</abbr>
```

address

```
<address> . . . </address>
```

Supplies the contact information for the document or an `article` in the document. It is not to be used for all postal addresses, unless the address is provided as the contact information for the author of the document.

Usage

Categories:
    Flow content, palpable content

Permitted contexts:
    Where flow content is expected

Permitted content:
    Flow content, but may not contain the following elements: `h1` through `h6`, `article`, `aside`, `nav`, `section`, `header`, `footer`, and `address`

Start/end tags:
    Required/Required

Attributes

HTML5 Global Attributes

Example

```
<address>
Contributed by <a href="http://example.com/authors
/robbins/"> Jennifer Robbins</a>, <a href="http://
www.oreilly.com/"> O'Reilly Media</a>
</address>
```

area

```
<area> (XHTML: <area/> or <area />)
```

The area element is used within the map element of a client-side image map to define a specific clickable ("hot") area.

Usage

Categories:
Flow content, phrasing content

Permitted contexts:
Where phrasing content is expected, but must be contained in a map element

Permitted content:
Empty

Start/end tags:
This is a *void* (empty) element, meaning it has only a start tag and may not have any contents. In HTML, the end tag is forbidden. In XHTML, the element must be closed with a trailing slash (`<area/>` or `<area />`).

Attributes

HTML5 Global Attributes

`alt="text"`
Required. Specifies a short description of the image that is displayed when the image file is not available.

`coords="values"`
Specifies a list of comma-separated pixel coordinates that define a "hot" area of an image map.

`download="file name"`
WHATWG and HTML5.1 only. Indicates the link is used for downloading a resource. The value is the name the resource file should be given on the local file system once it is downloaded.

`href="URI"`
Specifies the location of the document or resource that is accessed by clicking or tapping on the defined area.

`hreflang="language code"`
Not in HTML 4.01. Specifies the language of the target document.

media="all|aural|braille|handheld|print|projection|screen|
tty|tv"

> **Not in HTML 4.01. HTML5 only**. Describes the media for
> which the target document was designed. The default is all.
> This attribute has been removed in HTML5.1 and
> WHATWG.

ping="*URLs*"

> **WHATWG only**. Specifies a space-separated list of URLs that
> must be contacted when the link is followed, and is useful for
> user tracking.

rel="*link type keyword*"

> Describes one or more relationships from the current source
> document to the linked document. The link relationship types
> specified for area are alternate, author, bookmark, help,
> license, next, nofollow, noreferrer, prefetch, prev, search,
> and tag.

shape="rect|circle|poly|default"

> Defines the shape of the clickable area.

target="*text*"

> Specifies the name of the window or iframe in which the target
> document should be displayed.

type="*MIME type*"

> Specifies the media or content type (MIME type) of the linked
> content—for example, text/html.

Example (HTML)

See also map.

```
<map name="space">
  <area shape="rect" coords="203,23,285,106" href=http://
www.nasa.gov alt="">
  <area shape="rect" coords="203,23,285,106" href=http://
www.nasa.gov alt="">
</map>
```

article

`<article> . . . </article>`

Not in HTML 4.01. Represents a self-contained piece of content, such as a magazine article, blog post, reader comment, or newspaper article that is intended to be independently distributable, reusable, or used in syndication. `article` elements may be nested, such as for comments associated with a blog post.

Usage

Categories:
Flow content, sectioning content, palpable content

Permitted contexts:
Where flow content is expected

Permitted content:
Flow content (but no main element descendants)

Start/end tags:
Required/Required

Attributes

HTML5 Global Attributes

Example

```
<article>
  <header>
    <h1>Further Research</h1>
    <p><time datetime="2010-01-14T03:13">January 14, 2010
</time></p>
    <p>An introduction to the topic. . .</p>
  </header>
  <p>Content of the article starts. . .</p>
  <p>And another paragraph in the article.</p>
  <footer>Copyright &#169; 2013 Jane Author</footer>
</article>
```

aside

`<aside> . . . </aside>`

Not in HTML 4.01. Represents content that is tangentially related to the surrounding content (a section, article, or other content flow), such as pull quotes, lists of links, advertising, and other content typically presented as a sidebar.

Usage

Categories:
Flow content, sectioning content, palpable content

Permitted contexts:
Where flow content is expected

Permitted content:
Flow content (but with no main descendants)

Start/end tags:
Required/Required

Attributes

HTML5 Global Attributes

Example

```
<article>
  <h1>Important Experiment Findings</h1>
  <p>First paragraph . . .</p>
  <p>Second paragraph . . .</p>
  <aside>
    <h1>For Further Reading</h1>
    <ul>
      <li><a href="">Interesting Article</a></li>
      <li><a href="">Another Interesting Article</a></li>
    </ul>
  </aside>
</article>
```

audio

```
<audio> . . . </audio>
```

Not in HTML 4.01. Embeds a sound file media in the web page without requiring a plug-in. The content of the audio element can be used by agents that don't support the element. The audio file may be provided with the src attribute. More commonly, because different browsers support different audio formats, a series of file format options are provided with source elements contained in the audio element. Other fallback content may be provided in the audio element for nonsupporting browsers.

There is still debate regarding the supported audio format for the audio element. No file format is supported by all browsers. As of this writing, browser support for available file formats is as follows:

IE 9+ (versions prior to 9 do not support the audio element): MP3, MP4, and WebM

Chrome 5+: MP3, MP4, WAV, Ogg Vorbis, and WebM

Firefox 3.5+: WAV, Ogg Vorbis, and WebM (4+). MP3 and MP4 support will be added to Firefox but only when a third-party decoder is available.

Safari 4+ and Mobile Safari 3+: MP3, MP4, and WAV

Android (2.0+): MP3, WAV, Ogg Vorbis, and WebM (2.3.3+)

Usage

Categories:
Flow content, phrasing content, embedded content, interactive content (if it has a controls attribute), palpable content (if it has a controls attribute)

Permitted contexts:
Where embedded content is expected

Permitted content:
Transparent content, containing either a src attribute or one or more source elements, followed by either flow content or phrasing content. video or audio elements are not permitted.

Start/end tags:
Required/Required

Attributes

HTML5 Global Attributes

autoplay *(or* autoplay="autoplay" *in XHTML)*
> Plays the media file automatically.

controls *(or* controls="controls" *in XHTML)*
> Indicates that the user agent (browser) should display a set of playback controls for the media file.

crossorigin="anonymous|use-credentials"
> Indicates if the user agent must check for credentials for a media file that is coming from a URL with a different origin than the source document. The default is anonymous (no credentials needed).

loop *(or* loop="loop" *in XHTML)*
> Indicates that the media file should start playing again automatically once it reaches the end.

mediagroup="*text*"
> Links multiple media elements together by assigning them the same mediagroup value.

muted *(or* muted="muted" *in XHTML)*
> Disables (mutes) the audio output, even if it overrides user preferences.

preload="none|metadata|auto"
> Hints to the browser whether the media file should begin to load automatically based on anticipated best user experience. none prevents the preload; metadata does not download the media file, but does fetch the resource metadata; auto leaves the decision to preload to the user agent.

src="*URL*"
> Specifies the location of the media file.

Examples

See also source.

```
<audio src="soundtrack.webm" autoplay controls>
    Your browser does not support embedded audio.
    Listen to the file <a href="soundtrack.webm">here</a>.
</audio>
```

```
<audio id="soundtrack" controls preload="auto">
   <source src="soundtrack.mp3" type="audio/mp3">
   <source src="soundtrack.ogg" type="audio/ogg">
   <source src="soundtrack.webm" type="audio/webm">
</audio>
```

---

b

`<b> . . . </b>`

Words and phrases that need to stand out from the surrounding text without conveying added importance or emphasis, such as keywords or product names. In earlier HTML specifications, the b element was defined as bold.

Usage

Categories:
Flow content, phrasing content, palpable content

Permitted contexts:
Where phrasing content is expected

Permitted content:
Phrasing content

Start/end tags:
Required/Required

Attributes

HTML5 Global Attributes

Example

```
<li>Turn left onto <b>Blackstone Blvd.</b>.</li>
```

---

base

`<base>` (XHTML: `<base/>` or `<base />`)

Specifies the base pathname for all relative URLs in the document. Place this element within the head of the document.

Usage

Categories:
Metadata content

Permitted contexts:
In a head element that has no other base elements

Permitted content:
Empty

Start/end tags:
This is an empty (void) element, meaning it has only a start tag and may not have any contents. In HTML, the end tag is forbidden. In XHTML, the element must be closed with a trailing slash (<base/> or <base />).

Attributes

HTML5 Global Attributes

href ="*URI*"
Specifies the absolute URI that acts as the base URI for resolving relative URIs.

target ="*name*"
Defines the default target window or iframe for all links in the document.

Example (HTML)

```
<head>
    <title>Sample document</title>
    <base href="http://www.example.com/stories/">
</head>
```

bdi

```
<bdi> . . . </bdi>
```

Stands for "bidirectional isolation" and is used to indicate a selection of text that might read in a different direction from the surrounding text. It may be useful for names and comments added by users or text embedded from an outside source.

Usage

Categories:
Flow content, phrasing content, palpable content

Permitted contexts:
Where phrasing content is expected

Permitted content:
Phrasing content

Start/end tags:
Required/Required

Attributes

HTML5 Global Attributes

dir ="ltr|rtl|auto"
Specifies the direction of the text: ltr (left to right), rtl (right to left), or auto (determined by the user agent). In the bdi element, if the dir attribute is omitted, it defaults to auto and does not inherit from the parent.

Example

```
<ul>
  <li>User <bdi>jcranmer</bdi>: 12 posts.
  <li>User <bdi>hober</bdi>: 5 posts.
  <li>User <bdi>إيان</bdi>: 3 posts.
</ul>
```

[Example used with permission from the WHATWG HTML specification.]

---

bdo

```
<bdo> . . . </bdo>
```

Stands for "bidirectional override" and is used to indicate a selection of text that reads in the opposite direction than the surrounding text. For instance, in a left-to-right reading document, the bdo element may be used to indicate a selection of Hebrew text that reads right to left (rtl).

Usage

Categories:
Flow content, phrasing content, palpable content

Permitted contexts:
Where phrasing content is expected

Permitted content:
Phrasing content

Start/end tags:
Required/Required

Attributes

HTML5 Global Attributes

dir ="ltr|rtl|auto"
Specifies the direction of the text: ltr (left to right), rtl (right to left), or auto (determined by the user agent).

Example

```
<bdo dir="ltr">English phrase in otherwise Arabic text.
</bdo>
```

---

blockquote

```
<blockquote> . . . </blockquote>
```

Indicates a long quotation from another source. Its content is some number of block-level elements, such as paragraphs.

In HTML5, the blockquote element is also a *sectioning root*, meaning it indicates a section that may have its own outline. That means that heading levels used within blockquote elements will not contribute to the overall outline of the page.

Usage

Categories:
Flow content, sectioning root, palpable content

Permitted contexts:
Where flow content is expected

Permitted content:
> Flow content

Start/end tags:
> Required/Required

Attributes

HTML5 Global Attributes

`cite="URI"`
> Provides a link to information about the source from which the quotation was borrowed.

Example

```
<blockquote cite="http://www.example.com">
  <h1>Fascinating Evidence</h1>
  <p>This is the beginning of a lengthy quoted
      passage (text continues . . . ) </p>
  <p>And it is still going on and on
      (text continues . . . )</p>
</blockquote>
```

---

body

`<body> . . . </body>`

The body of a document contains the document's content. Content may be presented visually (as in a graphical browser window) or aurally (by a screen reader). There may only be one body element in a document. In HTML documents, it is optional; in XHTML, it is required.

Usage

Categories:
> Sectioning root

Permitted contexts:
> As the second element in an html element

Permitted content:
> Flow content

Start tag is optional if the element is empty or if the first thing in the body element is not a space character or a comment, except if the first thing inside the body element is a `script` or `style` element. The end tag is optional if the body element is not immediately followed by a comment. (XHTML: Required/Required)

Attributes

HTML5 Global Attributes; plus onafterprint, onbeforeprint, onbeforeunload, onblur, onerror, onfocus, onhashchange, onload, onmessage, onoffline, ononline, onpagehide, onpageshow, onpopstate, onresize, onscroll, onstorage, and onunload

Example

```
<!DOCTYPE HTML PUBLIC "-//W3C//DTD HTML 4.01//EN"
"http://www.w3.org/TR/HTML4.01/strict.dtd">
<html>
  <head>
    <title>Document Title</title>
  </head>
  <body>
    <p>Content of document . . . </p>
  </body>
</html>
```

---

br

`<br>` (XHTML: `<br/>` or `<br />`)

Represents a line break in the content, such as in a poem or postal address.

Usage

Categories:
Flow content, phrasing content

Permitted contexts:
Where phrasing content is expected

Permitted content:
Empty

This is an empty (void) element, meaning it has only a start tag and may not have any contents. In HTML, the end tag is forbidden. In XHTML, the element must be closed with a trailing slash (`<br/>` or `<br />`).

Attributes

HTML5 Global Attributes

Example (HTML)

```
<p>O'Reilly Media<br>
1005 Gravenstein Highway North<br>
Sebastopol, CA 95472</p>
```

---

button

```
<button> . . . </button>
```

Used as part of a form, defines a clickable button that functions similarly to buttons created with the `input` element but allows for richer rendering possibilities. Buttons can contain content such as text and images (but not image maps).

Usage

Categories:
Flow content, phrasing content, interactive content, "listed, labelable, and submittable form-associated element", palpable content

Permitted contexts:
Where phrasing content is expected

Permitted content:
Phrasing content, but may contain no interactive content

Start/end tags:
Required/Required

Attributes

HTML5 Global Attributes

`autofocus` *(`autofocus="autofocus"` in XHTML)*

> **Not in HTML 4.01**. Indicates the control should have focus (be highlighted and ready for user input) when the document loads.

`disabled` *(`disabled="disabled"` in XHTML)*

> Disables the control for user input. It can be altered only via a script. Browsers may display disabled controls differently (grayed out, for example), which could be useful for dimming certain controls until required info is supplied.

`form="id of the form owner"`

> **Not in HTML 4.01**. Explicitly associates the input control with its associated form (its *form owner*). With this method, the input control does not need to be a child of the `form` element that applies to it.

`formaction="URL"`

> **Not in HTML 4.01**. Specifies the application that will process the form. It is used only with a submit button (`input type="submit"`) and has the same function as the `action` attribute for the `form` element.

`formenctype="content type"`

> **Not in HTML 4.01**. Specifies how the form values are encoded with the `post` method type. It is used only with a submit button (`input type="submit"`) and has the same function as the `enctype` attribute for the `form` element. The default is Internet Media Type (`application/x-www-form-urlencoded`). The value `multipart/form-data` should be used in combination with the `file` input type. The value `text/plain` sets the MIME type of the submitted data to be text/plain.

`formmethod="get|post"`

> **Not in HTML 4.01**. Specifies which HTTP method will be used to submit the form data. It is used only with a submit button (`input type="submit"`) and has the same function as the `method` attribute for the `form` element.

formnovalidate="*URL*"
> **Not in HTML 4.01**. Indicates that the form is not to be validated during submission. It is used only with a submit button (input type="submit") and has the same function as the novalidate attribute for the form element (new in HTML5).

formtarget="*name*"
> **Not in HTML 4.01**. Specifies the target window for the form results. It is used only with a submit button (input type= "submit") and has the same function as the target attribute for the form element.

menu="*text*"
> **Not in HTML 4.01**. If the button's type attribute is set to menu, this attribute is required to provide the ID of a menu element on the same page with its type set to popup.

name="*text*"
> **Required**. Assigns the control name for the element.

type="submit|reset|button|menu"
> Identifies the behavior of the button: submit (submit button, the default type), reset (reset button), button (custom button controlled with JavaScript), or menu (shows a menu).

value="*text*"
> Assigns the value to the button control. The behavior of the button is determined by the type attribute.

Example

```
<button type="reset" name="reset"><img src="thumbs-down.
gif" alt="thumbs-down icon"> Try again.</button>
```

canvas

```
<canvas> . . . </canvas>
```

Not in HTML 4.01. Represents a two-dimensional area that can be used for rendering dynamic bitmap graphics, such as graphs, games, drawing programs, animations, and so on. The markup establishes a rectangular space on the page for the canvas. The image on the canvas is generated with scripting (usually JavaScript).

The canvas element is one of the better supported HTML5 features, with basic support in Firefox 2.0+, Safari 3.1+, Chrome 1.0+, Internet Explorer 9+, and Opera 9.0. The FlashCanvas JavaScript library (flashcanvas.net (*http://flashcanvas.net*)) can add canvas support to nonsupporting browsers using the Flash drawing API.

Usage

Categories:
> Flow content, phrasing content, embedded content, palpable content

Permitted contexts:
> Where embedded content is expected

Permitted content:
> Transparent, either phrasing or flow content

Start/end tags:
> Required/Required

Attributes

HTML5 Global Attributes

height="*number*"
> Specifies the height of the canvas area in CSS pixels.

width="*number*"
> Specifies the width of the canvas area in CSS pixels.

Example

```
<html>
<head>
  <script type="application/x-javascript">
function draw() {
  var canvas = document.getElementById("box");
  var ctx = canvas.getContext("2d");
  ctx.fillStyle = "rgb(163, 120, 240)";
  ctx.fillRect (55, 50, 75, 100);
}
  </script>
</head>
<body onload="draw()">
  <canvas id="box" width="250" height="250"></canvas>
```

```
    </body>
  </html>
```

---

caption

```
<caption> . . . </caption>
```

Provides a summary of a table's contents or purpose. The `caption` element must immediately follow the `table` start tag and precede all other table elements.

Note

If the `table` is the only content of a `figure`, use the `figcaption` element instead.

Usage

Categories:
  None

Permitted contexts:
  As the first child of a `table` element

Permitted content:
  Flow content, but may not contain `table` elements

Start/end tags:
  Required/Required

Attributes

HTML5 Global Attributes

Example

```
<table>
  <caption>A brief description of the data in this table.
  </caption>
  <tr>
    <td>data</td><td>data</td>
  </tr>
</table>
```

cite

`<cite> . . . </cite>`

Denotes the title of a work—a reference to another work, especially books, magazines, articles, TV shows, and so on.

Usage

Categories:
> Flow content, phrasing content, palpable content

Permitted contexts:
> Where phrasing content is expected

Permitted content:
> Phrasing content

Start/end tags:
> Required/Required

Attributes

HTML5 Global Attributes

Example

```
<p>Recipe from <cite>Food & Wine Magazine</cite>.</p>
```

---

code

`<code> . . . </code>`

Denotes a fragment of computer code that appears as an inline (phrasing) element. By default, visual browsers render code in a monospace font.

Usage

Categories:
> Flow content, phrasing content, palpable content

Permitted contexts:
> Where phrasing content is expected

Permitted content:
    Phrasing content

Start/end tags:
    Required/Required

Attributes

HTML5 Global Attributes

Example

```
<p>DOM reference: <code>document.getElementById</code></p>
```

---

col

`<col>` (XHTML: `<col/>` or `<col />`)

Establishes a column (or columns via the `span` attribute) within a table so that attribute properties may be applied to all the cells in the column(s). The `col` element does not group columns structurally (that is handled by the `colgroup` element) but rather is an empty element that allows attributes to be shared. The `col` element must appear after the `caption` element and before any row (`tr`) or row group (`thead`, `tbody`, `tfoot`) elements with the `table` element.

Usage

Categories:
    None

Permitted contexts:
    As the child of a `colgroup` element that doesn't have a `span` attribute

Permitted content:
    Empty

Start/end tags:
    This is an empty (void) element, meaning it has only a start tag and may not have any contents. In HTML, the end tag is forbidden. In XHTML, the element must be closed with a trailing slash (`<col/>` or `<col />`).

Attributes

HTML5 Global Attributes

span="*number*"
> Specifies the number of columns "spanned" by the col ele-
> ment. The default value is 1. All columns indicated in the span
> are formatted according to the attribute settings in col.

Example (HTML):

See also colgroup *and* table.

```
<table>
  <col span="2" width="100" class="name">
  <col span="1" width="50" class="date">
  <thead> . . .
  (markup continues)
```

---

colgroup

```
<colgroup> . . . </colgroup>
```

Defines a conceptual group of columns that form a structural division within a table. The colgroup element must appear after the
caption element and before any row (tr) or row group (thead, tbody,
tfoot) elements with the table element.

A table may include more than one column group. The number of
columns in a group is specified either by the value of the span attribute or by a tally of column (col) elements within the group.
Column groups may be useful in speeding table display (for example, the columns can be displayed incrementally without waiting
for the entire contents of the table) and provide a system for display
on nonvisual display agents such as speech- and Braille-based
browsers.

Usage

Categories:
> None

Permitted contexts:
> As a child of a table element, after any caption elements and
> before any thead, tbody, tfoot, and tr elements.

Permitted content:
> If it has a span attribute, then it is empty. If the span attribute is absent, then it should contain one or more col elements.

Start/end tags:
> The start tag is optional if it has col as its first child and it is not preceded by a colgroup start tag without an end tag. The end tag is optional if the colgroup is not immediately followed by a space character or comment. (XHTML: Required/ Required.)

Attributes

HTML5 Global Attributes

span="*number*"
> Specifies the number of columns "spanned" by the colgroup element. The default value is 1. All columns indicated in the span are formatted according to the attribute settings in colgroup.

Example

See also col.

```
<table>
  <colgroup id="employinfo">
    <col span="2" width="100">
    <col span="1" width="50" class="date">
  </colgroup>
  <thead> . . . (markup continues)
```

---

command

<command> (XHTML: <command/> or <command />)

HTML5 only. Used within a menu element, a command is an interactive element that represents an immediate action that can be triggered by the user (usually via onclick).

Notes

The command element has been replaced by the menuitem element in HTML5.1 and the WHATWG specification, and should not be used. See the menu and menuitem listings.

Usage

Categories:
> Metadata content, flow content, phrasing content

Permitted contexts:
> Where metadata content is expected; where phrasing content is expected

Permitted content:
> Empty

Start/end tags:
> This is an empty (void) element, meaning it has only a start tag and may not have any contents. In HTML, the end tag is forbidden. In XHTML, the element must be closed with a trailing slash (`<command/>` or `<command />`).

Attributes

HTML5 Global Attributes

checked *(checked="checked" in XHTML)*
> Indicates that a command is selected.

command="*id of master elememt*"
> When a command element uses the command attribute, its state is set based on the master command.

disabled *(disabled="disabled" in XHTML)*
> Indicates that a command is not available in the current state.

icon="*URL*"
> Specifies the location of an image to be used as a button for the command.

label="*text*"
> Provides the name of the command, as displayed to the user.

radiogroup="*text*"
> Specifies the name of a group of commands when the command type is set to radio.

title="*text*"
> Provides a hint describing the command to aid the user.

type="command|checkbox|radio"

Indicates the kind of command. The command keyword indicates a normal command with an associated action. checkbox indicates the command state can be toggled on or off. radio indicates the command represents the selection of one item from a list of items.

Example

Note: menuitem has replaced command in HTML5.1 and the living WHATWG spec.

```
<menu>
    <command onclick="cut()" label="Cut">
    <command onclick="copy()" label="Copy">
    <command onclick="paste()" label="Paste">
    <command onclick="delete()" label="Clear">
</menu>
```

(Comments)

```
<!-- . . . -->
```

Inserts notes or scripts into the document that are not displayed by the browser. Comments can be any length and are not restricted to one line.

Start/End Tags

Required/Required

Attributes

Not applicable.

Example

```
<!-- start secondary navigation here -->
<ul> . . . (markup continues)
```

data

```
<data> . . . </data>
```

WHATWG and HTML5.1 only. Provides a machine-readable equivalent for its content (via the value attribute) to be used for data processing. It may be used for all sorts of data, including dates, times, measurements, weights, microformats, and so on.

Usage

Categories:
> Flow content, phrasing content, palpable content

Permitted contexts:
> Where phrasing content is expected

Permitted content:
> Phrasing content

Start/end tags:
> Required/Required

Attributes

HTML5 Global Attributes

```
value="machine-readable value"
```
> Provides a machine-readable equivalent to the content of the element.

Example

```
<data value="12">Twelve</data>
<data value="2011-11-12">Last Saturday</data>
```

datalist

```
<datalist> . . . </datalist>
```

Not in HTML 4.01. Used with an input control set to the new list type, the datalist element creates a drop-down menu of pre-defined suggestions (via the option element), providing an "auto-complete" function as the user types in the field (called a *combobox*). The difference between datalist and select is that the user does not need to select one of the suggestions and can write anything in the field.

Usage

Categories:
    Flow content, phrasing content

Permitted contexts:
    Where phrasing content is expected

Permitted content:
    Either phrasing content or zero or more option elements

Start/end tags:
    Required/Required

Attributes

HTML5 Global Attributes

Example

```
<input type="text" list="flavors">
  <datalist id="flavors">
    <option value="Vanilla">
    <option value="Chocolate">
    <option value="Mango">
  </datalist>
```

dd

`<dd> . . . </dd>`

Denotes the description, definition, or value in a term/description pair within a description list (dl). The dd element must be used within the dl element and is preceded by either dt or dd. The dd element may contain other block-level elements.

Usage

Categories:
    None

Permitted contexts:
    After dt or dd elements inside dl elements

Permitted content:
    Flow content

Start/end tags:
    Required/Optional (XHTML: Required/Required)

Attributes

HTML5 Global Attributes

Example

```
<dl>
    <dt><code>em</code></dt>
    <dd>Indicates emphasized text.</dd>

    <dt><code>strong</code></dt>
    <dd>Denotes strongly emphasized text.</dd>
</dl>
```

---

del

```
<del> . . . </del>
```

Indicates text that has been removed from the document. It may be useful for legal documents and any instance where edits need to be tracked. Its counterpart is the inserted text element (`ins`). The del element may be used to indicate either inline or block-level elements.

Usage

Categories:
    Flow content, phrasing content

Permitted contexts:
    Where phrasing content is expected

Permitted content:
    Transparent (is derived from the content model of its parent)

Start/end tags:
    Required/Required

Attributes

HTML5 Global Attributes

`cite="URL"`

> Can be set to point to a source document that explains why the document was changed.

`datetime="YYYY-MM-DDThh:mm:ssTZD"`

> Specifies the date and time the change was made. Dates and times follow the format shown here, where YYYY is the four-digit year, MM is the two-digit month, DD is the day, hh is the hour (00 through 23), mm is the minute (00 through 59), and ss is the second (00 through 59). TZD stands for Time Zone Designator, and its value can be Z (to indicate UTC, Coordinated Universal Time), an indication of the number of hours and minutes ahead of UTC (such as +03:00), or an indication of the number of hours and minutes behind UTC (such as –02: 20).
>
> This is the standard format for date and time values in HTML. For more information, see *www.w3.org/TR/1998/ NOTE-datetime-19980827*.

Example

```
Chief Executive Officer: <del title="retired" datetime=
"2013-05-01T14:09:00EDT">Peter Pan</del> <ins>Pippi
Longstocking</ins>
```

---

details

`<details> . . . </details>`

Not in HTML 4.01. Represents a disclosure widget (an area that can be toggled open and closed) that reveals additional information or controls. The details element may contain a summary element that provides a summary or title for the details, followed by additional flow content. The details element should not be used for footnotes.

Notes

As of this writing, details and summary are only supported by Chrome 12+, Safari 6+, iOS Safari 6+ Android 4.0+ and Blackberry 10+.

Usage

Categories:
> Flow content, sectioning root, interactive content, palpable content

Permitted contexts:
> Where flow content is expected

Permitted content:
> One summary element followed by flow content

Start/end tags:
> Required/Required

Attributes

HTML5 Global Attributes

open *(open="open" in XHTML)*
> Specifies that the details should be in the open or revealed state when the document loads.

Example

See also summary.

```
<details>
  <summary>Additional information</summary>
  <ul>
  <li>This is some information about the author the user
    might be interested in reading.</li>
  <li>This is even more relevant information.</li>
  </ul>
</details>
```

dfn

```
<dfn> . . . </dfn>
```

Indicates the defining instance of the enclosed term. It can be used to call attention to the introduction of special terms and phrases or to reference them later in the document.

Usage

Categories:
    Flow content, phrasing content, palpable content

Permitted contexts:
    Where phrasing content is expected

Permitted content:
    Phrasing content, but may not contain dfn descendants

Start/end tags:
    Required/Required

Attributes

HTML5 Global Attributes

Example

```
<dfn>Truecolor</dfn> uses 24 bits per pixel.
```

dialog

```
<dialog> . . . </dialog>
```

WHATWG and HTML5.1 only. Represents a floating dialog box, such as log-in windows, UI hints, lightboxes, and other pop-up or modal content that requires user interaction. When the dialog element is open, the rest of the page is inactive (inert).

Notes

As of this writing, no browsers support the dialog element.

Usage

Categories:
Flow content, sectioning root

Permitted contexts:
Where flow content is expected

Permitted content:
Flow content

Start/end tags:
Required/Required

Attributes

HTML5 Global Attributes

open *(open="open" in XHTML)*
Specifies that the dialog element is active and the user can interact with it.

Example

```
<dialog id="login" draggable="true">
  <p>You need to be logged in to post a comment</p>
  <button>Log In</button>
  <button>No thanks</button>
<dialog>
```

---

div

```
<div> . . . </div>
```

Denotes a generic "division" or container for content within the flow of the document. Elements contained within a div are treated as a semantic group. The div element is typically given meaning with the class, id, title, or lang attributes, which also allow it to be accessible to scripts and selected in stylesheets.

Usage

Categories:
Flow content, palpable content

Permitted contexts:
> Where flow content is expected

Permitted content:
> Flow content

Start/end tags:
> Required/Required

Attributes

HTML5 Global Attributes

Example

```
<div id="summary">
  <h1>In Closing</h1>
  <p>We can summarize as follows...</p>
</div>
```

---

dl

```
<dl> . . . </dl>
```

Indicates a description list (also called an association list). Each item in the list is name-value pair consisting of a name (**dt**) and its value (**dd**). Description lists may be used for terms and definitions, questions and answers, or any other groups of name-value data. There may be multiple **dt** elements for a **dd** or vice versa (see Examples).

Note

The dl element was defined as a "definition list" in HTML 4.01.

Usage

Categories:
> Flow content, palpable content (if the element's children contain at least one name-value pair)

Permitted contexts:
> Where flow content is expected

Permitted content:
> Zero or more groups, each consisting of one or more **dt** elements followed by one or more **dd** elements

---

Start/end tags:
    Required/Required

Attributes

HTML5 Global Attributes

Examples

```
<dl>
  <dt>Serif</dt>
  <dd>Times, Times New Roman, Georgia</dd>

  <dt>Sans-serif</dt>
  <dd>Arial, Verdana, Helvetica</dd>

  <dt>Monospace</dt>
  <dd>Courier, Andale Mono, Lucida Console</dd>
</dl>

<dl>
  <dt>Authors</dt>
  <dd>John</dd>
  <dd>Jane</dd>
...
</dl>

<dl>
  <dt lang="en-US"><dfn>color</dfn></dt>
  <dt lang="en-GB"><dfn>colour</dfn></dt>
  <dd> A sensation which (in humans) derives from the
ability of  the fine structure of the eye to distinguish
three differently filtered analyses of a view. </dd>
</dl>
```

---

dt

`<dt> . . . </dt>`

Denotes the name portion of an item within a description list. The
dt element may only include inline (phrasing) content.

Usage

Categories:
    None

Permitted contexts:
> Before dd or dt elements inside dl elements

Permitted content:
> Flow content, but may not contain header, footer, article, aside, nav, section, or h1–h6

Start/end tags:
> Required/Optional (XHTML: Required/Required)

HTML5 Global Attributes

Example

```
<dl>
  <dt>Serif</dt>
  <dd>Times, Times New Roman, Georgia</dd>

  <dt>Sans-serif</dt>
  <dd>Arial, Verdana, Helvetica</dd>

  <dt>Monospace</dt>
  <dd>Courier, Andale Mono, Lucida Console</dd>
</dl>
```

---

em

```
<em> . . . </em>
```

Indicates text that should be stressed or emphasized (typically indicated stylistically with italic text).

Usage

Categories:
> Flow content, phrasing content, palpable content

Permitted contexts:
> Where phrasing content is expected

Permitted content:
> Phrasing content

Start/end tags:
> Required/Required

Attributes

HTML5 Global Attributes

Example

```
<p><em>Simon</em> is an excellent craftsman.</p>

<p>Simon is an <em>excellent</em> craftsman.</p>
```

---

embed

<embed> (XHTML: <embed/> or <embed />)

Not in HTML 4.01. Embeds an object into the web page. Embedded objects are most often multimedia files that use plug-in technology for playback (for example, Flash movies, QuickTime movies, and the like). In addition to the attributes listed below, certain media types and their respective plug-ins may have proprietary attributes for controlling the playback of the file.

Notes

Although commonly supported by browsers, the embed element was not part of the HTML 4.01 or earlier specifications (in favor of the object element for embedded media); however, it has been added to the HTML5. Because it was supported but not documented, it has many browser- and media-specific attributes, and its syntax is not clear. Many developers use both object and embed for a single media object for backward compatibility, even though it does not conform to the standard.

Usage

Categories:
> Flow content, phrasing content, embedded content, interactive content, palpable content

Permitted contexts:
> Where embedded content is expected

Permitted content:
> Empty

Start/end tags:

In HTML5, embed is specified as an empty element with no closing tag. Modern browsers generally support embed with a closing tag as well.

HTML5 Attributes

HTML5 Global Attributes

Note: Some plug-ins require their own proprietary attributes for the embed element. Read the documentation for the media type you are trying to embed.

height="*number*"

Specifies the height of the object in number of pixels. Some media types require this attribute.

src="*URL*"

Provides the location of the resource to be placed on the page.

type="*media (MIME) type*"

Specifies the MIME type of the media in order to load the appropriate plug-in. The suffix of the file name given as the source may also be used to determine which plug-in to use.

width="*number*"

Specifies the width of the object in number of pixels. Some media types require this attribute.

Example (HTML5)

```
<embed src="movies/vacation.mov" width="240" height="196"
type="video/quicktime">
```

Nonstandard example with end tag

```
<embed src="movies/vacation.mov" width="240" height="196"
pluginspage="http://www.apple.com/quicktime/download/">
<noembed><img src="vacation.gif"> You do not seem to have
the plugin.</noembed>
</embed>
```

fieldset

`<fieldset>` . . . `</fieldset>`

Establishes a group of related form controls and labels. `fieldset` elements are placed within the `form` element. It was introduced to improve form accessibility for users with alternative browsing devices. The name of the `fieldset` is provided by the first child `legend` element. `fieldset` elements may be nested.

Usage

Categories:
> Flow content, sectioning root, "listed, form-associated element", palpable content

Permitted contexts:
> Where flow content is expected

Permitted content:
> An optional `legend` element, followed by flow content

Start/end tags:
> Required/Required

Attributes

HTML5 Global Attributes

`disabled` *(`disabled="disabled"` in XHTML)*
> **Not in HTML 4.01**. Disables the controls contained in the `fieldset`. It can be altered only via a script. Browsers may display disabled controls differently (grayed out, for example), which could be useful for dimming certain controls until required info is supplied.

`form="`*id of the form owner*`"`
> **Not in HTML 4.01**. Explicitly associates the fieldset with its associated form (its *form owner*). With this method, the field set does not need to be a child of the form element that applies to it.

`name="`*text*`"`
> **Not in HTML 4.01**. Assigns a name to the `fieldset`.

Example

```
<form>
<fieldset id="customer">
 <legend>Customer contact information</legend>
 <label>Full name <input type="text" name="name">
 </label>
 <label>Email Address <input type="text" name="email">
 </label>
 <label>State <input type="text" name="state"></label>
</fieldset>
</form>
```

figcaption

`<figcaption> . . . </figcaption>`

Not in HTML 4.01. Represents a caption or legend for its parent figure element.

Usage

Categories:
    None

Permitted contexts:
    As the first or last child of a figure element

Permitted content:
    Flow content

Start/end tags:
    Required/Required

Attributes

HTML5 Global Attributes

Examples

```
<figure>
  <img src="piechart.png" alt="2014 sales chart">
  <figcaption>Sales skyrocket in 2014</figcaption>
</figure>
```

figure

```
<figure> . . . </figure>
```

Not in HTML 4.01. Indicates some set of self-contained content
that is referred to from the main content, such as illustrations, code
examples, diagrams, and poems. A caption may be provided for the
figure with the optional figcaption element, which may come at
the beginning or end of the figure markup.

Usage

Categories:
> Flow content, sectioning root, palpable content

Permitted contexts:
> Where flow content is expected

Permitted content:
> Flow content, with an optional figcaption element at the be-
> ginning or end

Start/end tags:
> Required/Required

Attributes

HTML5 Global Attributes

Examples

```
<figure>
  <img src="piechart.png" alt="2014 sales chart">
  <figcaption>Sales skyrocket in 2014</figcaption>
</figure>

<figure>
<figcaption>Sample CSS Rule</figcaption>
<pre><code>
body {
  background-color: #369;
  color: white;
}
  </code></pre>
</figure>
```

footer

`<footer> . . . </footer>`

Not in HTML 4.01. Represents information associated with and typically found at the bottom of a document, article, or section, such as copyright, publication date, author information, or a list of related links. There is no requirement that the footer come at the end of the section or document. It could come at or near the beginning if that makes semantic sense.

Usage

Categories:
Flow content, palpable content

Permitted contexts:
Where flow content is expected

Permitted content:
Flow content, but it may not contain header, footer, or main elements

Start/end tags:
Required/Required

Attributes

HTML5 Global Attributes

Examples

```
<article>
    <h1>How to Etch Glass</h1>
    <p>Start with clean glass...</p>
    ... markup continues...
    <footer>Copyright &copy; 2013 Jennifer Robbins</footer>
</article>
```

form

`<form> . . . </form>`

Indicates an interactive form that contains controls for collecting user input as well as other page content. There may be more than

one form in a document, but forms may not be nested inside one
another, and it is important that they do not overlap.

Usage

Categories:
> Flow content, palpable content

Permitted contexts:
> Where flow content is expected

Permitted content:
> Flow content, but it may not contain other form elements

Start/end tags:
> Required/Required

Attributes

HTML5 Global Attributes

`accept-charset="charset list"`
> Specifies the list of character encodings for input data that
> must be accepted by the server to process the current form.
> The value is a space- and/or comma-delimited list of ISO char-
> acter set names. The default value is `unknown`. This attribute is
> not widely supported.

`action="URL"`
> **Required**. Specifies the URL of the application that will pro-
> cess the form. The default is the current URL.

`autocomplete="on|off"`
> **Not in HTML 4.01**. Allows the user agent (browser) to fill in
> a field automatically (`on`) or requires the user to enter the in-
> formation every time (`off`).

`enctype="content type"`
> Specifies how the values for the form controls are encoded
> when they are submitted to the server when the method is
> `post`. The default is the Internet Media Type (`application/x-
> www-form-urlencoded`). The value `multipart/form-data` should
> be used in combination with the `file` input element. The new
> `text/plain` value sets the MIME type to text/plain.

method="GET|POST"

> Specifies which HTTP method will be used to submit the form data. With get (the default), the information is appended to and sent along with the URL itself.

name="*text*"

> Assigns a name to the form.

novalidate *(novalidate="novalidate" in XHTML)*

> **Not in HTML 4.01**. Indicates that the form is not to be validated during submission.

target="*name*"

> Specifies a target for the results of the form submission to be loaded so that results of a form can be displayed in another window or iframe. The special target values _bottom, _top, _parent, and _self may be used.

Example

```
<form action="/mailinglist.php" method="POST">
<fieldset>
<legend>Join Our Mailing List</legend>
<ol>
<li><label>Name: <input type="text" name="username">
</label></li>
<li><label>Password: <input type="text" name="pswd">
</label></li>
</ol>
</fieldset>
</form>
```

h1, h2, h3, h4, h5, h6

<h*n* > . . . </h*n* >

Specifies a heading that briefly describes the section it introduces. There are six levels of headings, from h1 (most important) to h6 (least important). HTML syntax requires that headings appear in order (for example, an h2 should not precede an h1) for proper document structure. Doing so not only improves accessibility, but aids in search engine optimization (information in higher heading levels is given more weight).

Note

In HTML5, heading order can be repeated within sections of the same document, allowing greater flexibility with heading levels. This is to aid the outlining of documents and allows sections of a document to fall into the outline correctly no matter which document the section appears in. The HTML5 outline algorithm is not well supported as of this writing.

Usage

Categories:
    Flow content, heading content, palpable content

Permitted contexts:
    Where flow content is expected

Permitted content:
    Phrasing content

Start/end tags:
    Required/Required

Attributes

HTML5 Global Attributes

Example

```
<h1>Story Title</h1>
<p>In the beginning ... </p>
<h2>Subsection Title</h2>
<p>And so on ... </p>
<p>And so on ... </p>
```

---

head

```
<head> . . . </head>
```

Contains information about the document, a collection of metadata. Every head element must include a title element that provides a description of the document. The head element may also include any of these elements in any order: base, link, meta, noscript, script, and style. The head element merely acts as a container of these elements and does not have any content of its own.

Usage

Categories:
   None

Permitted contexts:
   As the first element in an html element

Permitted content:
   Zero or more elements of metadata content (base, command, link, meta, noscript, script, style, title) with exactly one title element. If the document is an iframe srcdoc, the title element is not required.

Start/end tags:
   Optional/Optional (XHTML: Required/Required)

Attributes

HTML5 Global Attributes

Example

```
<!DOCTYPE html>
<html>
  <head>
    <title>Document Title</title>
    <style type="text/css">h1 {color: #333;}</style>
  </head>
  <body>
    <p>Content of document . . . </p>
  </body>
</html>
```

header

```
<header> . . . </header>
```

Not in HTML 4.01. Represents information that goes at the beginning of a section, most often the headline, but the header may also include navigation links, advertising, introductions, etc. It may contain any flow content except header or footer elements.

Usage

Categories:
    Flow content, palpable content

Permitted contexts:
    Where flow content is expected

Permitted content:
    Flow content, but it may not contain **header** or **footer** elements

Start/end tags:
    Required/Required

Attributes

HTML5 Global Attributes

Examples

```
<body>
<header>
  <nav><ul><li>About</li><li>Home</li></ul></nav>
  <h1>White Rabbits</h1>
  <p>Welcome to the White Rabbits fan site.</p>
</header>
<h2>Rabbit Sightings</h2>... markup continues ...
</body>
```

---

hgroup

`<hgroup> . . . </hgroup>`

Not in HTML 4.01 or HTML5.1. Used to group a stack of h1–h6 headings so that subsequent heading levels are treated as subheads or taglines and do not contribute to the outline structure of the page.

Note

The hgroup element has been flagged for removal from HTML5. It is included here merely to duplicate the state of the HTML5 spec as of this writing, but it is considered obsolete due to lack of implementation and should not be used.

Usage

Categories:
Flow content, heading content, palpable content

Permitted contexts:
Where flow content is expected

Permitted content:
One or more h1, h2, h3, h4, h5, and/or h6 elements

Start/end tags:
Required/Required

Attributes

HTML5 Global Attributes

Example

```
<hgroup>
  <h1>Web Design in a Nutshell</h1>
  <h2>A Desktop Quick Reference</h2>
</hgroup>
```

---

hr

`<hr>` (XHTML: `<hr/>` or `<hr />`)

Indicates a paragraph-level thematic break, or an indication that one topic or thought has completed and another one is beginning.

Usage

Categories:
Flow content

Permitted contexts:
Where flow content is expected

Permitted content:
Empty

Start/end tags:
> This is an empty (void) element, meaning it has only a start tag and may not have any contents. In HTML, the end tag is forbidden. In XHTML, the element must be closed with a trailing slash (`<hr/>` or `<hr />`).

Attributes

HTML5 Global Attributes

Example (HTML)

```
<p>These are notes from Thursday.</p>
<hr>
<p>These are notes from Friday.</p>
```

---

html

`<html> . . . </html>`

This is the root element of HTML (and XHTML) documents, meaning all other elements are contained within it. The html element has no ancestors. The opening `<html>` tag is placed at beginning of the document, just after the document type declaration. The closing tag goes at the end of the document. If the tags are omitted, html is still implied as the root element.

Notes

It is recommended that the language of the document be provided with the `lang` attribute.

Usage

Categories:
> None

Permitted contexts:
> As the root of the document

Permitted content:
> A head element followed by a body element

Start/end tags:
> Optional/Optional; XHTML: Required/Required

HTML5 Global Attributes

manifest=`"URL"`
> **Not in HTML 4.01**. Points to a cache used with the offline web application API.

xmlns=`"http://www.w3.org/1999/xhtml"`
> **Required for XHTML only**. In an XHTML document, this declares the XML namespace for the document.

Example (HTML5)

```
<!DOCTYPE html>
<html lang="en">
  <head>
    <title>Document Title</title>
  </head>
  <body>
    <p>Content of document . . . </p>
  </body>
</html>
```

Example (XHTML)

```
<!DOCTYPE html PUBLIC "-//W3C//DTD XHTML 1.0
Transitional//EN"
 "http://www.w3.org/TR/xhtml1/DTD/xhtml1-transitional
.dtd">
<html xmlns="http://www.w3.org/1999/xhtml" xml:lang="en"
lang="en">
  <head>
    <title>Document Title</title>
  </head>
  <body>
    <p>Content of document . . . </p>
  </body>
</html>
```

---

i

`<i> . . . </i>`

Indicates that the text is in a different voice or mood than the surrounding text, such as a phrase from another language, a technical phrase, or a thought. In older specifications, i was defined as italic text.

Usage

Categories:
    Flow content, phrasing content, palpable content

Permitted contexts:
    Where phrasing content is expected

Permitted content:
    Phrasing content

Start/end tags:
    Required/Required

Attributes

HTML5 Global Attributes

Example

```
The Western Black Widow Spider, <i>Latrodectus hesperus</i>,
is commonly found . . .
```

---

iframe

```
<iframe> . . . </iframe>
```

Defines an inline frame that is used for embedding an HTML document in a separate browsing context (window) nested within the parent document. An inline frame displays the content of an external document and may display scrolling devices if the content doesn't fit in the specified window area. Inline frames may be positioned similarly to images.

Usage

Categories:
    Flow content, phrasing content, embedded content, interactive content, palpable content

Permitted contexts:
    Where embedded content is expected

Permitted content:
> Text content. If using an algorithm, the resulting output must be a list of nodes without parsing errors or scripts and may only contain phrasing content.

Start/end tags:
> Required/Required

Attributes

HTML5 Global Attributes

allowfullscreen
> **Not in HTML 4.01**. Indicates that the objects in the iframe are allowed to use requestFullScreen().

height="*number*"
> Specifies the height of the inline frame in pixels or as a percentage of the window size.

name="*text*"
> Assigns a name to the inline frame to be referenced by targeted links.

sandbox="allow-forms | allow-pointer-lock | allow-popups |
allow-same-origin | allow-scripts | allow-top-navigation"
> **Not in HTML 4.01**. Used to enable scripts, pop ups, plugins, and form submission in embedded documents.

seamless *(seamless="seamless" in XHTML)*
> **Not in HTML 4.01**. Makes the browser treat the embedded document as though it were part of the parent document for purposes of link targets, document structure, and CSS inheritance.

src="*URL*"
> Specifies the URL address of the HTML document to display initially in the inline frame.

srcdoc="*HTML content*"
> **Not in HTML 4.01**. Specifies actual HTML content to appear in the iframe.

```
width="number"
```
Specifies the width of the inline frame in pixels or as a per-
centage of the window size. Internet Explorer and Navigator
use a default width of 300 pixels.

Example

```
<h1>Inline (Floating) Frames</h1>
<iframe src="ads.html" width="300" height="200"><iframe>
```

---

img

`<img>` (XHTML: `<img/>` or `<img />`)

Represents an image in the content flow. The `src` and `alt` attributes
are required.

Usage

Categories:
> Flow content, phrasing content, embedded content, palpable
> content, interactive content if it has a `usemap` attribute

Permitted contexts:
> Where embedded content is expected

Permitted content:
> Empty

Start/end tags:
> This is an empty (void) element, meaning it has only a start
> tag and may not have any contents. In HTML, the end tag is
> forbidden. In XHTML, the element must be closed with a
> trailing slash (`<img/>` or `<img />`).

Attributes

HTML5 Global Attributes

```
alt="text"
```
> **Required**. Provides a string of alternative text that appears
> when the image is not or cannot be displayed.

`crossorigin="anonymous|use-credentials "`

> **Not in HTML 4.01**. On a site that allows cross-origin access files, this attribute indicates if requests from other domains must present credentials to access the image.

`height="number"`

> Specifies the height of the image in pixels. It is not required, but is recommended to speed up the rendering of the web page.

`ismap (ismap="ismap" in XHTML)`

> Indicates that the graphic is used as the basis for a server-side *image map* (an image containing multiple hypertext links).

`src="URL"`

> **Required**. Provides the location of the graphic file to be displayed.

`srcset="image candidate string"`

> **WHATWG only**. Allows authors to specify alternative images for different viewport sizes and higher pixel densities. The value is a comma-separated list of image locations with a descriptor that specifies the device requirements for its use. For example, `srcset="image-HD.jpg 2x, image-phone.jpg 240w"` instructs user agents to use *image-HD.jpg* if the display has double pixel density (such as the Apple Retina display) and to use *image-phone.png* if the device width is up to 240 pixels.

`usemap="URL"`

> Specifies the map containing coordinates and links for a *client-side image map* (an image containing multiple hypertext links).

`width="number"`

> Specifies the width of the image in pixels. It is not required but is recommended to speed up the rendering of the web page.

Example

```
<p>Your ideal pet: <img src="pig.gif" alt="A pig"></p>
```

input

`<input>` (XHTML: `<input/>` or `<input />`)

The **input** element is used to create a variety of form input controls. The type of control is defined by the **type** attribute. Following is a complete list of attributes (with descriptions) that can be used with the **input** element. Not all attributes can be used with all control types. The attributes associated with each control type are listed below.

Usage

Categories:
> Flow content, phrasing content. If the **type** attribute is *not* in the Hidden state, then interactive content, palpable content, as well as "listed, labelable, submittable, and resettable form-associated content." If the **type** attribute is in the Hidden state, then "listed, submittable, and resettable form-associated content."

Permitted contexts:
> Where phrasing content is expected

Permitted content:
> Empty

Start/end tags:
> This is an empty (void) element, meaning it has only a start tag and may not have any contents. In HTML, the end tag is forbidden. In XHTML, the element must be closed with a trailing slash (`<input/>` or `<input />`).

Attributes

HTML5 Global Attributes

`accept="MIME type"`
> Specifies a comma-separated list of content types that a server processing the form will handle correctly. It can be used to filter out nonconforming files when prompting a user to select files to send to the server. Applies to the **file** input type only.

`alt="text"`
> Specifies alternative text for an image used as a button. Applies to the image input type.

`autocomplete="on|off"`
> **Not in HTML 4.01**. Allows the user agent (browser) to fill in a field automatically (on) or requires the user to enter the information every time (off). Omitting this attribute causes the control to inherit the autocomplete setting for the associated form element. Applies to input types text, password, email, tel, search, url, number, range, date, time, datetime, datetime-local, month, week, and color.

`autofocus (autofocus="autofocus" in XHTML)`
> **Not in HTML 4.01**. Indicates the control should have focus (be highlighted and ready for user input) when the document loads. Applies to all input types.

`checked (checked="checked" in XHTML)`
> When this attribute is added to a radio button or checkbox input, the input will be checked when the page loads. Applies to the checkbox and radio input types.

`dirname="text string"`
> **Not in HTML 4.01**. Enables the submission of the directionality of the element (ltr or rtl) by providing the name of the field that contains the value. This could enable a form to have a user-selected direction setting for form entries. Applies to the text and search input types.

`disabled (disabled="disabled" in XHTML)`
> Disables the control for user input. It can be altered only via a script. Browsers may display disabled controls differently (grayed out, for example), which could be useful for dimming certain controls until required information is supplied. Applies to all input types.

`form="id of the form owner"`
> **Not in HTML 4.01**. Explicitly associates the input control with its associated form (its *form owner*). With this method, the input control does not need to be a child of the applicable form element. Applies to all input types.

`formaction="URL"`

> **Not in HTML 4.01**. Specifies the application that will process the form. It is used only with a submit button (`type="submit"` or `"image"`) and has the same function as the `action` attribute for the `form` element.

`formenctype="content type"`

> **Not in HTML 4.01**. Specifies how the form values are encoded with the post method type. It is used only with a submit button (`type="submit"` or `"image"`) and has the same function as the `enctype` attribute for the `form` element. The default is Internet Media Type (`application/x-www-form-urlencoded`). The value `multipart/form-data` should be used in combination with the `file` input type. The `text/plain` value sets the MIME type to `text/plain`.

`formmethod="get|post"`

> **Not in HTML 4.01**. Specifies which HTTP method will be used to submit the form data. It is used only with a submit button (`type="submit"` or `"image"`) and has the same function as the `method` attribute for the `form` element.

`formnovalidate` *(`formnovalidate="formnovalidate"` in XHTML)*

> **Not in HTML 4.01**. Indicates that the form is not to be validated during submission. It is used only with a submit button (`type="submit"` or `"image"`) and has the same function as the `novalidate` attribute for the `form` element.

`formtarget="name"`

> **Not in HTML 4.01**. Specifies the target window for the form results. It is used only with a submit button (`type="submit"` or `"image"`) and has the same function as the `target` attribute for the `form` element.

`height="number of pixels"`

> **Not in HTML 4.01**. Specifies the height of the button image when the input type is set to `image`.

`inputmode="verbatim|latin|latin-name|latin-prose|`
`full-width-latin|kana|katakana|numeric|tel|email|url"`

> **Not in HTML 4.01**. Indicates what kind of input mechanism would be most helpful for users entering content into the form control. Applies to the `text` and `search` input types.

---

list="*id of datalist*"

> **Not in HTML 4.01**. Indicates that the control has a list of predefined suggestions for the user, which are provided by a datalist element. The value of the list attribute is the id of the associated datalist. Applies to input types text, email, tel, search, url, number, range, date, time, datetime-local, datetime, month, week, and color.

max="*number or string*"

> **Not in HTML 4.01**. Specifies the upper boundary of the accepted value range for the element. The max value must not be less than the min value. Applies to input types number, range, date, time, datetime, datetime-local, month, and week.

maxlength="*number*"

> Specifies the maximum number of characters the user can enter for input elements set to text, password, email, search, tel, or url.

min="*number or string*"

> **Not in HTML 4.01**. Specifies the lower boundary of the accepted value range for the element. The min value defines the base for step operations. Applies to input types number, range, date, time, datetime, datetime-local, month, and week.

multiple (multiple="multiple" *in XHTML)*

> **Not in HTML 4.01**. Indicates the user is allowed to specify more than one value. Applies to file and email input types.

name="*text*"

> Assigns a name to the control; a script program uses this name to reference the control.

pattern="*JavaScript regular expression*"

> **Not in HTML 4.01**. Specifies a regular expression against which the control's value is to be checked. This is useful for making sure user input matches the format of the expected value, for example, a telephone number or an email address. The title attribute can be used with pattern to provide a description of the expected pattern/format of the input. Applies to text, password, email, tel, search, and url input types.

placeholder="*number*"
> **Not in HTML 4.01.** Provides a short (one word or short phrase) hint or example to help the user enter the correct data or format. If a longer description is necessary, use the title attribute. Applies to text, password, email, tel, search, and url input types.

readonly (readonly="readonly" *in XHTML*)
> Indicates that the form input may not be modified by the user. Applies to text, password, email, tel, search, url, number, date, time, datetime, datetime-local, month, and week.

required (required="required" *in XHTML*)
> **Not in HTML 4.01.** When present, indicates the input value is required. Applies to text, password, checkbox, radio, file, email, tel, search, url, number, date, time, datetime, datetime-local, month, and week.

size="*number*"
> Specifies the width of a text-entry control, measured in number of characters. Users may type entries that are longer than the space provided, causing the field to scroll to the right. Applies to text, password, email, tel, search, and url,

src="*URL*"
> When the input type is image, this attribute provides the location of the image to be used as a push button.

step="any/*number*"
> **Not in HTML 4.01.** Indicates the granularity that is expected and required of the value by limiting the allowed value to permitted units. The value of this attribute is dependent on the type of the input control. It may be a number greater than zero or the keyword any, which allows any unit value. Applies to number, range, date, time, datetime, datetime-local, month, and week.

type="button|checkbox|color|date|time|datetime|
datetime-local|email|file|hidden|image|month|number|
password|radio|range|reset|search|submit|tel|text|url|week"
> Specifies the data type and associated form control. Descriptions of each input type and their associated attributes are listed below.

`value="text"`

> Specifies the initial value for this control. Applies to all input types except image.

`width="number of pixels"`

> **Not in HTML 4.01**. Specifies the width of the bottom image when the input type is set to image.

input type = "button"

Creates a customizable "push" button. Customizable buttons have no specific behavior but can be used to trigger functions created with JavaScript controls. Data from `type="button"` controls is never sent with a form when a form is submitted to the server; these button controls are for use only with script programs on the browser:

```
<input type="button" value="Push Me!">
```

HTML5 Global Attributes

autofocus (autofocus="autofocus" in XHTML) (**Not in HTML 4.01**)

disabled (disabled="disabled" in XHTML)

form="*id of the form owner*" (**Not in HTML 4.01**)

name="*text*"

value="*text*"

input type = "checkbox"

Creates a checkbox input element within a form. Checkboxes are like on/off switches that the user can toggle. Several checkboxes in a group may be selected at one time. When a form is submitted, only the "on" checkboxes submit values to the server:

```
<p>Which of the following operating systems have you
used?</p>
<ul>
<li><input type="checkbox" name="os" value="Win">Windows
</li>
<li><input type="checkbox" name="os" value="Linux"
    checked>Linux</li>
<li><input type="checkbox" name="os" value="OSX"
    checked>Macintosh OSX</li>
```

```
<li><input type="checkbox" name="os" value="DOS">DOS</li>
</ul>
```

HTML5 Global Attributes

autofocus (autofocus="autofocus" in XHTML) (**Not in HTML 4.01**)

checked (checked="checked" in XHTML)

disabled (disabled="disabled" in XHTML)

form="*id of the form owner*" (**Not in HTML 4.01**)

name="*text*"

required (required="required" in XHTML) (**Not in HTML 4.01**)

value="*text*"

input type="color"
This input type is not valid in HTML 4.01.

Creates a color picker control for selecting a color value:

```
<input type="color" name="background" value="3D458A">
```

HTML5 Global Attributes

autocomplete="on|off"

autofocus (autofocus="autofocus" in XHTML)

disabled (disabled="disabled" in XHTML)

form="*id of form owner*"

list="*id of datalist*"

name="*name*"

value="*text*"

input type="date"
This input type is not valid in HTML 4.01.

Creates a date input control, such as a pop-up calendar, for specifying a date (year, month, day) with no time zone. The initial value must be provided in ISO date format:

```
<input type="date" name="birthday" value="2004-01-14">
```

HTML5 Global Attributes

autocomplete="on|off"

autofocus (autofocus="autofocus" in XHTML)

disabled (disabled="disabled" in XHTML)

form="*id of form owner*"

list="*id of datalist*"

max="*number or string*"

min="*number or string*"

name="*name*"

readonly (readonly="readonly" in XHTML)

required (required="required" in XHTML)

step="any|*number*"

value="*YYYY-MM-DD*"

input type= "datetime"

This input type is not valid in HTML 4.01.

Creates a combined date/time input control. The value is an ISO formatted date and time that is defined and submitted as UTC time (equivalent to GMT):

```
<input type="datetime" name="post" value=
"2004-01-14T03:13:00-5:00">
```

HTML5 Global Attributes

autocomplete="on|off"

autofocus (autofocus="autofocus" in XHTML)

disabled (disabled="disabled" in XHTML)

form="*id of form owner*"

list="*id of datalist*"

max="*number or string*"

min="*number or string*"

name="*name*"

readonly (readonly="readonly" in XHTML)

required (required="required" in XHTML)

step="any|*number*"

value="*YYYY-MM-DDThh:mm:ssTZD*"

input type="datetime-local"

This input type is not valid in HTML 4.01.

Creates a combination date/time input control, assuming the time is in the local time zone. Initial values must be provided in ISO date/time format:

```
<input type="datetime-local" name="post" value=
"2009-06-23T13:44:16:00">
```

HTML5 Global Attributes

autocomplete="on|off"

autofocus (autofocus="autofocus" in XHTML)

disabled (disabled="disabled" in XHTML)

form="*id of form owner*"

list="*id of datalist*"

max="*number or string*"

min="*number or string*"

name="*name*"

readonly (readonly="readonly" in XHTML)

required (required="required" in XHTML)

step="any|*number*"

value="*YYYY-MM-DDThh:mm:ss*"

input type="email"

This input type is not valid in HTML 4.01.

Creates a text input for entering one or more email addresses. The user agent may look for patterns to confirm the entry is in email address format:

```
<input type="email" name="address" value="jn@example.com">
```

HTML5 Global Attributes

autocomplete="on|off"

autofocus (autofocus="autofocus" in XHTML)

disabled (disabled="disabled" in XHTML)

form="*id of form owner*"

list="*id of datalist*"

maxlength="*number*"

multiple (multiple="multiple" in XHTML)

pattern="*JavaScript regular expression*"

placeholder="*text*"

name="*name*"

readonly (readonly="readonly" in XHTML)

required (required="required" in XHTML)

size="*number*"

value="*text*"

input type="file"

Allows users to submit external files with their form submissions by providing a browsing mechanism in the form:

```
<form enctype="multipart/form-data">
<p>Send this file with my form information:<br>
  <input type="file" name="attachment" size="28">
</p>
</form>
```

HTML5 Global Attributes

accept="*MIME type*"

autofocus (autofocus="autofocus" in XHTML) (**Not in HTML 4.01**)

disabled (disabled="disabled" in XHTML)

form="*id of form owner*" (**Not in HTML 4.01**)

multiple (multiple="multiple" in XHTML) (**Not in HTML 4.01**)

name="*text*"

required (required="required" in XHTML) (**Not in HTML 4.01**)

input type="hidden"

Creates a control that does not display in the browser. Hidden controls can be used to pass special form-processing information to the server that the user cannot see or alter:

```
<input type="hidden" name="productID" value="12-XL">
```

HTML5 Global Attributes

disabled (disabled="disabled" in XHTML) (**Not in HTML 4.01**)

form="*id of form owner*" (**Not in HTML 4.01**)

name="*text*" (**Required**)

value="*text*" (**Required**)

input type="image"

Allows an image to be used as a substitute for a submit button. If a type="image" button is pressed, the form is submitted:

```
<input type="image" src="graphics/send.gif" alt="Send me">
```

HTML5 Global Attributes

alt="*text*"

autofocus (autofocus="autofocus" in XHTML) (**Not in HTML 4.01**)

disabled (disabled="disabled" in XHTML)

form="*id of form owner*" (**Not in HTML 4.01**)

formaction="*URL*" (**Not in HTML 4.01**)

formenctype="*content type*" (**Not in HTML 4.01**)

formmethod="get|post" (**Not in HTML 4.01**)

formnovalidate (formnovalidate="formnovalidate" in XHTML) (**Not in HTML 4.01**)

formtarget="*name*" (**Not in HTML 4.01**)

height="*number of pixels*" (**Not in HTML 4.01**)

name="*text*"

src="*URL*"

width="*number of pixels*" (**Not in HTML 4.01**)

input type="month"
This input type is not valid in HTML 4.01.

Creates a date input control, such as a pop-up calendar, for specifying a particular month in a year:

```
<input type="month" name="expires" value="2009-09">
```

HTML5 Global Attributes

autocomplete="on|off"

autofocus (autofocus="autofocus" in XHTML)

disabled (disabled="disabled" in XHTML)

form="*id of form owner*"

list="*id of datalist*"

max="*number or string*"

min="*number or string*"

name="*name*"

readonly (readonly="readonly" in XHTML)

required (required="required" in XHTML)

step="any|*number*"

value=" *YYYY-MM*"

input type="number"
This input type is not valid in HTML 4.01.

Creates a control (a text field or spinner) for specifying a numerical value:

```
<input type="number" name="price" min="100000"
max="300000" step="10000">
```

HTML5 Global Attributes

autocomplete="on|off"

autofocus (autofocus="autofocus" in XHTML)

disabled (disabled="disabled" in XHTML)

form="*id of form owner*"

list="*id of datalist*"

max="*number*"

min="*number*"

name="*name*"

placeholder="*text string*"

readonly (readonly="readonly" in XHTML)

required (required="required" in XHTML)

step="any|*number*"

value="*text or number string*"

input type= "password"

Creates a text input element (like <input type="text">), but the input text is rendered in a way that hides the characters, such as by displaying a string of asterisks or bullets. Note that this does *not* encrypt the information entered and should not be considered to be a real security measure:

```
<input type="password" name="password" size="8"
maxlength="8" value="abcdefg">
```

HTML5 Global Attributes

autocomplete="on|off" (**Not in HTML 4.01**)

autofocus (autofocus="autofocus" in XHTML) (**Not in HTML 4.01**)

disabled (disabled="disabled" in XHTML)

form="*id of form owner*" (**Not in HTML 4.01**)

maxlength="*number*"

name="*text*"

pattern="*JavaScript regular expression*" (**Not in HTML 4.01**)

placeholder="*text*" (**Not in HTML 4.01**)

readonly (readonly="readonly" in XHTML)

required (required="required" in XHTML) (**Not in HTML 4.01**)

size="*number*"

value="*text*"

input type="radio"

Creates a radio button that can be turned on and off. When a number of radio buttons share the same control name, only one button within the group can be "on" at one time, and all the others are "off." This makes them different from checkboxes, which allow multiple choices to be selected within a group. Only data from the "on" radio button is sent when the form is submitted:

```
<p>Which of the following operating systems do you like
best?</p>
<ul>
<li><input type="radio" name="os" value="Win">Windows</li>
<li><input type="radio" name="os" value="Linux">Linux</li>
<li><input type="radio" name="os" value="OSX" checked>
Macintosh OSX</li>
<li><input type="radio" name="os" value="DOS">DOS</li>
</ul>
```

HTML5 Global Attributes

checked (checked="checked" in XHTML)

autofocus (autofocus="autofocus" in XHTML) (**Not in HTML 4.01**)

disabled (disabled="disabled" in XHTML)

form="*id of form owner*" (**Not in HTML 4.01**)

name="*text*" (**Required**)

required (required="required" in XHTML) (**Not in HTML 4.01**)

value="*text*" (**Required**)

input type="range"

This input type is not valid in HTML 4.01.

Creates a slider control that a user can employ to enter a value that does not need to be precise. The range starts at the value provided by the min attribute (0 by default) and ends at the value provided by the max attribute (100 by default):

```
<input type="range" name="satisfaction" min="0" max="10">
```

HTML5 Global Attributes

autocomplete="on|off"

autofocus (autofocus="autofocus" in XHTML)

disabled (disabled="disabled" in XHTML)

form="*id of form owner*"

list="*id of datalist*"

max="*number*"

min="*number*"

name="*name*"

step="any|*number*"

value="*text*"

input type="reset"

Creates a reset button that clears the contents of the elements in a form (or sets them to their default values):

```
<input type="reset" value="Start Over">
```

HTML5 Global Attributes

autofocus (autofocus="autofocus" in XHTML) (**Not in HTML 4.01**)

disabled (disabled="disabled" in XHTML)

form="*id of form owner*" (**Not in HTML 4.01**)

name="*text*"

value="*text*"

input type="search"

This input type is not valid in HTML 4.01.

Creates a one-line text input control for entering a search query:

```
<input type="search" name="srch" size="25"
value="Search term">
```

HTML5 Global Attributes

autocomplete="on|off"

autofocus (autofocus="autofocus" in XHTML)

disabled (disabled="disabled" in XHTML)

dirname="*text string*"

form="*id of form owner*"

inputmode="verbatim|latin|latin-name|latin-prose|
full-width-latin|kana|katakana|numeric|tel|email|url"

list="*id of datalist*"

maxlength="*number*"

name="*name*"

pattern="*JavaScript regular expression*"

placeholder="*text*"

readonly (readonly="readonly" in XHTML)

required (required="required" in XHTML)

size="*number*"

value="*text*"

input type="submit"

Creates a submit button control. Pressing the button immediately sends the information in the form to the server for processing:

```
<p>You have completed the form.</p>
<p><input type="submit"></p>
```

HTML5 Global Attributes

autofocus (autofocus="autofocus" in XHTML) (**Not in HTML 4.01**)

disabled (disabled="disabled" in XHTML)

form="*id of form owner*" (**Not in HTML 4.01**)

formaction="*URL*" (**Not in HTML 4.01**)

formenctype="*content type*" (**Not in HTML 4.01**)

formmethod="get|post " (**Not in HTML 4.01**)

formnovalidate (formnovalidate="formnovalidate" in XHTML) (**Not in HTML 4.01**)

formtarget="*name*" (**Not in HTML 4.01**)

name="*text*"

value="*text*"

input type="tel"

This input type is not valid in HTML 4.01.

Creates an input control for entering and editing a telephone number:

```
<input type="tel" name="homeno" value="000-000-0000">
```

HTML5 Global Attributes

autocomplete="on|off"

autofocus (autofocus="autofocus" in XHTML)

disabled (disabled="disabled" in XHTML)

form="*id of form owner*"

list="*id of datalist*"

maxlength="*number*"

name="*name*"

pattern="*JavaScript regular expression*"

placeholder="*text*"

readonly (readonly="readonly" in XHTML)

required (required="required" in XHTML)

size="*number*"

value="*text*"

input type="text"

Creates a text input element. This is the default input type, as well as one of the most useful and common. Text provided for the value attribute will appear in the text control when the form loads:

```
<input type="text" name="username" size="15"
maxlength="50" value="enter your name">
```

HTML5 Global Attributes

autocomplete="on|off" (**Not in HTML 4.01**)

autofocus (autofocus="autofocus" in XHTML) (**Not in HTML 4.01**)

disabled (disabled="disabled" in XHTML)

dirname="*text string*" (**Not in HTML 4.01**)

form="*id of form owner*" (**Not in HTML 4.01**)

inputmode="verbatim|latin|latin-name|latin-prose|
full-width-latin|kana|katakana|numeric|tel|email|url" (**Not in HTML 4.01**)

list="*id of datalist*" (**Not in HTML 4.01**)

maxlength="*number*"

name="*name*"

pattern="*JavaScript regular expression*" (**Not in HTML 4.01**)

placeholder="*text*" (**Not in HTML 4.01**)

readonly (readonly="readonly" in XHTML)

required (required="required" in XHTML) (**Not in HTML 4.01**)

size="*number*"

value="*text*"

input type="time"

This input type is not valid in HTML 4.01.

Creates a date input control for specifying a time (hour, minute, seconds, and fractional seconds) with no time zone indicated:

```
<input type="time" name="currenttime" value="23:15:00">
```

HTML5 Global Attributes

autocomplete="on|off"

autofocus (autofocus="autofocus" in XHTML)

disabled (disabled="disabled" in XHTML)

form="*id of form owner*"

list="*id of datalist*"

max="*number or string*"

min="*number or string*"

name="*name*"

readonly (readonly="readonly" in XHTML)

required (required="required" in XHTML)

step="any|*number*"

value="*hh:mm:ss*"

input type="url"

This input type is not valid in HTML 4.01.

Creates a text entry control for entering a single absolute URL. The user agent may validate the data entered to ensure it is in proper URL format and return an error message if it doesn't match:

```
<input type="url" name="blog" size="25"
value="http://www.example.com">
```

HTML5 Global Attributes

autocomplete="on|off"

autofocus (autofocus="autofocus" in XHTML)

disabled (disabled="disabled" in XHTML)

form="*id of form owner*"

list="*id of datalist*"

maxlength="*number*"

name="*name*"

pattern="*JavaScript regular expression*"

placeholder="*text*"

readonly (readonly="readonly" in XHTML)

required (required="required" in XHTML)

size="*number*"

value="*text*"

input type="week"

This input type is not valid in HTML 4.01.

Creates a date input control, such as a pop-up calendar, for specifying a particular week in a year. Values are provided in ISO week numbering format:

```
<input type="week" name="thisweek" value="2009-W34">
```

HTML5 Global Attributes

autocomplete="on|off"

autofocus (autofocus="autofocus" in XHTML)

disabled (disabled="disabled" in XHTML)

form="*id of form owner*"

list="*id of datalist*"

max="*number or string*"

min="*number or string*"

name="*name*"

readonly (readonly="readonly" in XHTML)

required (required="required" in XHTML)

```
step="any|number"
value="YYYY-W#"
```

___

ins

```
<ins> . . . </ins>
```

Indicates text that has been inserted into the document. It may be useful for legal documents and any instance in which edits need to be tracked. Its counterpart is deleted text (del). The ins element may indicate either inline or block-level elements; however, when used as an inline element (as within a p), it may not insert block-level elements because that would violate nesting rules.

Usage

Categories:
> Flow content, phrasing content, palpable content

Permitted contexts:
> Where phrasing content is expected

Permitted content:
> Transparent (derives from content model of parent element)

Start/end tags:
> Required/Required

Attributes

HTML5 Global Attributes

```
cite="URL"
```
> Can be set to point to a source document that explains why the document was changed.

```
datetime="YYYY-MM-DDThh:mm:ssTZD"
```
> Specifies the date and time the change was made. See the del element listing for an explanation of the date/time format.

Example

```
<li>Chief Executive Officer: <del title="retired">Peter Pan
</del> <ins>Pippi Longstocking</ins></li>
```

___

kbd

`<kbd>` . . . `</kbd>`

Stands for "keyboard" and indicates text (or voice input) entered by the user.

Usage

Categories:
> Flow content, phrasing content, palpable content

Permitted contexts:
> Where phrasing content is expected

Permitted content:
> Phrasing content

Start/end tags:
> Required/Required

Attributes

HTML5 Global Attributes

Example

```
<p>Enter your coupon code. Example: <kbd>AX4003</kbd></p>
```

keygen

`<keygen>` (XHTML: `<keygen/>` or `<keygen />`)

Not in HTML 4.01. Used as part of a form to generate key pairs that are used in web-based certificate management systems (for secure transactions).

Usage

Categories:
> Flow content, phrasing content, interactive content, palpable content, and "listed, labelable, submittable, and resettable form-associated element"

Permitted contexts:
> Where phrasing content is expected

Permitted content:
>   Empty

Start/end tags:
>   This is an empty (void) element, meaning it has only a start tag and may not have any contents. In HTML, the end tag is forbidden. In XHTML, the element must be closed with a trailing slash (`<keygen/>` or `<keygen />`).

Attributes

HTML5 Global Attributes

`autofocus` *(`autofocus="autofocus"` in XHTML)*
>   Indicates the control should be active and ready for user input when the document loads.

`challenge="challenge-string"`
>   Provides a challenge string to be submitted with the key.

`disabled` *(`disabled="disabled"` in XHTML)*
>   Prevents the control from being interactive and prevents its value from being submitted.

`form="id of form owner"`
>   Associates the element with a named `form` on the page.

`keytype="keyword"`
>   Identifies the type of key to be generated, for example, `rsa` or `ec`.

`name="text"`
>   Gives the control an identifying name for the form submission process.

Example

The following is based on an example from *developer.mozilla.org*, used with permission via a Creative Commons "Attribution-Share Alike" License:

```
<form method="post" action="http://www.example.com/
cgi-bin/decode.cgi">
   <keygen name="RSA public key" challenge="123456789"
       keytype="RSA">
```

```
    <input type="submit" name="createcertificate"
        value="Make Key">
</form>
```

label

`<label> . . . </label>`

Used to attach information to controls. Each label element is associated with exactly one form control. The label element may contain the form control, or it may use the for attribute to identify the control by its id value.

Usage

Categories:
> Flow content, phrasing content, interactive content, form-associated element, palpable content

Permitted contexts:
> Where phrasing content is expected

Permitted content:
> Phrasing content, but may not contain labelable elements unless it is the element's labeled control and no descendent label elements.

Start/end tags:
> Required/Required

Attributes

HTML5 Global Attributes

`for="text"`
> Explicitly associates the label with the control by matching the value of the for attribute with the value of the id attribute within the control element.

`form="id of the form owner"`
> Explicitly associates the label element with its associated form (its *form owner*). With this method, the label does not need to be the child of the applicable form element.

Examples

Form control and its labeling text contained within the label element:

```
<label>Last Name: <input type="text" size="32"></label>
```

Using the for/id method to associate the form control with its labeling text:

```
<label for="lastname">Last Name:</label>
<input type="text" id="lastname" size="32">
```

---

legend

```
<legend> . . . </legend>
```

Assigns a caption to a fieldset (it must be the first child of a field set element). This improves accessibility when the fieldset is rendered nonvisually.

Usage

Categories:
    None

Permitted contexts:
    As the first child of a fieldset element

Permitted content:
    Phrasing content

Start/end tags:
    Required/Required

Attributes

HTML5 Global Attributes

Example

```
<fieldset>
  <legend>Mailing List Sign-up</legend>
  <ul>
  <li><label>Add me to your mailing list
       <input type="radio" name"list"></label></li>
```

```
<li><label>No thanks <input name"list" value="no">
    </label></li>
  </ul>
</fieldset>
```

---

li

`<li> . . . </li>`

Defines an item in a list. It is used within the ol and ul list elements.

Usage

Categories:
> None

Permitted contexts:
> Inside ol, ul, and menu elements.

Permitted content:
> Flow content

Start/end tags:
> Required/Optional (XHTML: Required/Required)

Attributes

HTML5 Global Attributes

value="*number*"
> Specifies an item's number when the li is part of an ordered
> list (ol). The following list items increase from the specified
> number.

Example

```
<ol>
  <li>Preheat oven to 300.</li>
  <li>Wrap garlic in foil.</li>
  <li>Bake for 2 hours.</li>
</ol>
```

link

`<link>` (XHTML: `<link/>` or `<link />`)

Defines the relationship between the current document and another document. Although it can signify such relationships as index, next, and previous, it is most often used to link a document to an external style sheet.

Usage

Categories:
Metadata content (if the `itemprop` attribute is present, where phrasing content is expected)

Permitted contexts:
Where metadata content is expected; in a `noscript` element that is a child of a `head` element; if the `itemprop` attribute is present, where phrasing content is expected

Permitted content:
Empty

Start/end tags:
This is an empty (void) element, meaning it has only a start tag and may not have any contents. In HTML, the end tag is forbidden. In XHTML, the element must be closed with a trailing slash (`<link/>` or `<link />`).

Attributes

HTML5 Global Attributes

`crossorigin="anonymous|use-credentials"`
Not in HTML 4.01. On a site that allows cross-origin access files, this attribute indicates whether requests from other domains must present credentials.

`href="URL"`
Identifies the linked document.

`hreflang="language code"`
Specifies the base language of the linked document.

```
media="all|screen|print|handheld|projection|tty|tv|
projection|braille|aural"
```
>Identifies the media to which the linked resource applies. Most often, it is used to assign stylesheets to their appropriate media.

```
rel="link type keyword"
```
>Describes one or more relationships from the current source document to the linked document. The link relationship types specified for link are alternate, author, help, icon, license, next, prefetch, prev, search, stylesheet, and tag.

```
sizes="any|two pixel measurements"
```
>**HTML5 only**. Specifies dimensions for icons when the rel of the link is set to icon.

```
type="resource"
```
>Shows the media or content type of a linked resource. The value text/css indicates that the linked document is an external Cascading Style Sheet.

Example

```
<head>
<link rel="stylesheet" href="/pathname/stylesheet.css">
</head>
```

---

main

```
<main> . . . </main>
```

WHATWG and HTML5.1 only. Represents the main content area of the body of a document. There may only be one main element in a document, and it may not be the child of an article, aside, footer, header, or nav elements.

Usage

Categories:
>Flow content, palpable content

Permitted contexts:
>Where flow content is expected (may not be contained in article, aside, footer, header, or nav elements)

Permitted content:
> Flow content

Start/end tags:
> Required/Required

Attributes

HTML5 Global Attributes

Example

```
<body>
<header>
  <h1>White Rabbits Fan Site</h1>
  <nav><ul> ... </ul></nav>
</header>
<main>
  <h2>Tour Dates</h2>
  <ul>
    <li>Providence, RI</li>
    <li>Brooklyn, NY</li>
  </ul>
... content continues...
</main>
</body>
```

---

map

`<map> . . . </map>`

Specifies a client-side image map. It contains some number of **area** elements that establish clickable regions within the image map.

Usage

Categories:
> Flow content, phrasing content, palpable content

Permitted contexts:
> Where phrasing content is expected

Permitted content:
> Transparent (derived from the content model of its parent)

Start/end tags:
    Required/Required

Attributes

HTML5 Global Attributes

id="*text*"
    Required in XHTML. Gives the map a unique name so that
    it can be referenced from a link, script, or style sheet.

name="*text*"
    Required. Gives the image map a name that is then referenced
    within the img element.

Example

```
<map name="space" id="space">
  <area shape="rect" coords="203,23,285,106"
    href=http://www.nasa.gov alt="">
  <area shape="circle" coords="372,64,40"
    href="mypage.html" alt="">
</map>
```

---

mark

<mark> . . . </mark>

Not in HTML 4.01. Represents a selection of text that has been
marked or highlighted for reference purposes or to bring it to the
attention of the reader. Marked text is considered to be of particular
relevance to the user.

Usage

Categories:
    Flow content, phrasing content, palpable content

Permitted contexts:
    Where phrasing content is expected

Permitted content:
    Phrasing content

Start/end tags:
    Required/Required

Attributes

HTML5 Global Attributes

Example

In this example, a user's search query ("estate tax") is marked in the returned document:

```
<p> ... PART I. ADMINISTRATION OF THE GOVERNMENT. TITLE IX.
TAXATION. CHAPTER 65C. MASS. <mark>ESTATE TAX</mark>.
Chapter 65C: Sect. 2. Computation of <mark>estate
tax</mark>.</p>
```

---

menu

```
<menu> . . . </menu>
```

Represents a list of interactive options or commands such as a menu of options in a web application. When the menu is a pop-up menu, its contents are one or more menuitem elements. In the HTML5 Candidate Recommendation, an option in a menu is provided by the command element, but the more forward looking HTML5.1 draft and the living WHATWG specification have replaced command with menuitem.

Note

In HTML 4.01, the deprecated menu element indicates a menu list, which consists of one or more list items (li). Menus were intended for a list of short choices, such as a menu of links to other documents.

Usage

Categories:
> Flow content; if the type element is in the toolbar state, then palpable content.

Permitted contexts:
> Where flow content is expected. If the type=popup, then as the child of a menu element that is in the pop-up state.

Permitted content:
> If type=toolbar, flow content or zero or more li elements. If type=popup, zero or more menuitem elements, zero or more hr elements, and zero or more menu elements with type=popup.

Start/end tags:
> Required/Required

Attributes

HTML5 Global Attributes

label="*text*"
> **Not in HTML 4.01.** Specifies a label for the menu, which can be displayed in nested menus.

type="popup|toolbar"
> **Not in HTML 4.01.** Identifies the kind of menu being declared. popup indicates a pop-up menu or a menu for a button with its type set to menu in a form. toolbar indicates the menu is to be used as a toolbar that can be interacted with immediately. If the type attribute is omitted, the default is merely a list of commands.

Example (HTML5.1 and WHATWG)

```
<menu type="popup">
    <menuitem onclick="cut()" label="Cut">
    <menuitem onclick="copy()" label="Copy">
    <menuitem onclick="paste()" label="Paste">
    <menuitem onclick="delete()" label="Clear">
</menu>
```

menuitem

<menuitem> (XHTML: <menuitem/> or <menuitem />)

Not in HTML 4.01. WHATWG and HTML5.1 only. Represents a command that can be chosen from a pop-up menu.

Usage

Categories:
> None

Permitted contexts:
> As a child of a menu element whose type attribute is in the pop-up menu state

Permitted content:
> Empty

Start/end tags:
> This is an empty (void) element, meaning it has only a start tag and may not have any contents. In HTML, the end tag is forbidden. In XHTML, the element must be closed with a trailing slash (`<menuitem/>` or `<menuitem />`).

Attributes

HTML5 Global Attributes

`checked` (`checked="checked"` *in XHTML*)
> Indicates that the command is selected. May be used only when type is set to `checkbox` or `radio`.

`command="`*id of the master command*`"`
> References a `menuitem` command that was defined and set elsewhere in the document or application.

`default` (`default="default"` *in XHTML*)
> Indicates the command is the default function for the menu.

`disabled` (`disabled="disabled"` *in XHTML*)
> Specifies the command is not available.

`icon="`*URL*`"`
> Specifies the location of an image that represents the command.

`label="`*text string*`"`
> Provides the name for the command as shown in the menu.

`radiogroup="`*text string*`"`
> Provides a name for a group of commands with their type set to `radio`. It may not be used with other `menuitem` types.

`type="command|checkbox|radio"`
> Indicates the type of command, either a normal command with an associated action (`command`) or an option that can be

toggled (checkbox), or a selection of one item from a list of items (radio).

Example

```
<menu>
    <menuitem onclick="cut()" label="Cut">
    <menuitem onclick="copy()" label="Copy">
    <menuitem onclick="paste()" label="Paste">
    <menuitem onclick="delete()" label="Clear">
</menu>
```

---

meta

<meta> (XHTML: <meta/> or <meta />)

Provides additional information (metadata) about the document. It should be placed within the head of the document. It is commonly used to identify its media type and character set. It can also provide keywords, author information, descriptions, and other metadata. The head element may contain more than one meta element.

Usage

Categories:
Metadata content; If itemprop is present, then flow and phrasing content

Permitted contexts:
In the head element or a noscript element in a head element. If the name (*http://www.w3.org/TR/html5/document-metadata .html#attr-meta-name*) attribute is present: where metadata content (*http://www.w3.org/TR/html5/dom.html#metadata -content-0*) is expected. If the itemprop attribute is present, where metadata or phrasing content is expected.

Permitted content:
Empty

Start/end tags:
This is an empty (void) element, meaning it has only a start tag and may not have any contents. In HTML, the end tag is forbidden. In XHTML, the element must be closed with a trailing slash (<meta/> or <meta />).

Attributes

HTML5 Global Attributes

charset="*character set*"
> **Not in HTML 4.01**. Can be used with the meta element as a
> substitute for the http-equiv method for declaring the char-
> acter set of the document.

content="*text*"
> **Required**. Specifies the value of the meta element property
> and is always used in conjunction with name, http-equiv, or
> itemprop.

http-equiv="content-language|content-type|default-style|
refresh|set-cookie"
> The specified information is treated as though it were included
> in the HTTP header that the server sends ahead of the docu-
> ment. It is used in conjunction with the content attribute (in
> place of the name attribute).

name="*text*"
> Specifies a name for the meta information property. Some de-
> fined names include application-name, author, description,
> generator, and keywords.

Example (HTML)

```
<meta charset="UTF-8">

<meta name="author" content="Jennifer Robbins">

<meta http-equiv="content-type" content="text/html;
charset=UTF-8">

<meta http-equiv="refresh" content= "15">
```

---

meter

```
<meter> . . . </meter>
```

Not in HTML 4.01. Represents a fractional value or a scalar measurement within a known range (also known as a *gauge*). It should
not be used to indicate progress (such as a progress bar) or when
there is no known maximum value.

Usage

Categories:
> Flow content, phrasing content, labelable element, palpable content

Permitted contexts:
> Where phrasing content is expected

Permitted content:
> Phrasing content (may not contain other `meter` elements)

Start/end tags:
> Required/Required

Attributes

HTML5 Global Attributes

`high="number"`
> Indicates the range that is considered to be "high" for the gauge

`low="number"`
> Indicates the range that is considered to be "low" for the gauge

`max="number"`
> Specifies the maximum or highest value of the range

`min="number"`
> Specifies the minimum or lowest value of the range

`optimum="number"`
> Indicates the range that is considered to be "optimum" for the gauge

`value="number"`
> Specifies the actual or "measured" value for the gauge

Examples

The following examples show three methods for indicating a measurement of 50%:

```
<meter>50%</meter>
<meter min="0" max="200">100</meter>
<meter min="0" max="200" value="100"></meter>
```

nav

`<nav>` . . . `</nav>`

Not in HTML 4.01. Represents a section of the document intended for navigation. Not all lists of links are appropriate for nav, only those that represent major navigation blocks on a page or within a section. The links within a nav element can be to other documents or to other areas within the current document.

Usage

Categories:
    Flow content, sectioning content, palpable content

Permitted contexts:
    Where flow content is expected

Permitted content:
    Flow content (may not contain main elements)

Start/end tags:
    Required/Required

Attributes

HTML5 Global Attributes

Example

```
<nav>
  <ul>
    <li><a href="">About us</a></li>
    <li><a href="">Contact</a></li>
    <li><a href="">Home</a></li>
  </ul>
</nav>
```

noscript

`<noscript>` . . . `</noscript>`

Provides alternate content when a script cannot be executed. The content of this element may be rendered if the user agent doesn't support scripting, if scripting support is turned off, or if the browser doesn't recognize the scripting language. When noscript appears in the head of a document and scripting is disabled, it may only contain link, style, and meta elements.

Notes

noscript is not to be used in the XML syntax of HTML5 because the element relies on an HTML parser.

Usage

Categories:
> Metadata content, flow content, phrasing content

Permitted contexts:
> In a head element if there are no ancestor noscript elements. Where phrasing content is expected if there are no ancestor noscript elements.

Permitted content:
> When scripting is disabled and the element is in a head element, it may contain in any order, zero or more link elements, style elements, and/or meta elements. When scripting is disabled and it is not in a head element, it is transparent (content model is derived from parent element) but it must not contain any noscript elements. Otherwise, it may have text content.

Start/end tags:
> Required/Required

Attributes

HTML5 Global Attributes

Example

```
<script type="text/JavaScript">
... script here
</script>
<noscript>
  <p>This function requires JavaScript to be enabled.</p>
</noscript>
```

object

`<object> . . . </object>`

A generic element used for embedding an external resource (such as an image, applet, movie, or audio) on a web page. The attributes required for the object element vary with the type of content it is placing. The embedded content may be treated as an image, a nested browsing context, or may be processed by a plug-in. The object element may contain content that will be rendered if the object cannot be embedded. The object element may also contain a number of param elements that pass important information to the object when it displays or plays. Not all objects require additional parameters. The object and param elements work together to allow authors to specify three types of information:

- The implementation of the object—that is, the executable code that runs in order to render the object.

- The data to be rendered. The data attribute specifies the location of the resource, in most cases an external file, such as a movie or a PDF.

- Additional settings required by the object at runtime. Some embedded media objects require additional settings that get called into play when the object plays or is rendered.

Usage

Categories:
> Flow content, phrasing content, embedded content, interactive (if it has a usemap attribute), palpable content, "listed, submittable, form-associated element"

Permitted contexts:
> Where embedded content is expected

Permitted content:
> Zero or more param elements, then flow content and/or interactive content

Start/end tags:
> Required/Required

Attributes

HTML5 Global Attributes

data="*URI*"
> Specifies the address of the resource. The syntax depends on the object.

form="*form id*"
> **Not in HTML 4.01**. Associates the object with a form element on the page.

height="*number*"
> Specifies the height of the object in pixels.

name="*text*"
> Specifies the name of the object to be referenced by scripts on the page.

type="*media type*"
> Specifies the media type of the resource.

typemustmatch (typemustmatch="typemustmatch" *in XHTML*)
> **Not in HTML 4.01**. Indicates that the resource indicated by the data attribute is only to be used if the value of the type attribute and the content type of the resource match.

usemap="*URL*"
> Specifies an image map to use with the object.

width="*number*"
> Specifies the object width in pixels.

Example

```
<object width="640" height="360"
type="application/x-shockwave-flash"
data="flash_player.swf">
  <param name="movie" value="flash_player.swf">
  <param name="flashvars" value="controlbar=over&amp;
  image=poster.jpg&amp;
          file=yourmovie-main.mp4">
  <img src="poster.jpg" width="640" height="360" alt=""
  title="No video playback capabilities, please download
  the video below">
</object>
```

ol

`<ol> . . . </ol>`

Defines an ordered (numbered) list that consists of one or more list items (li). The user agent inserts item numbers automatically.

Usage

Categories:
> Flow content; if its children include at least one li element, then palpable content

Permitted contexts:
> Where flow content is expected

Permitted content:
> Zero or more li elements

Start/end tags:
> Required/Required

Attributes

HTML5 Global Attributes

`reversed` (reversed="reversed" *in XHTML*)
> **Not in HTML 4.01**. Reverses the numbering sequence, from highest to lowest value.

`start="number"`
> Starts the numbering of the list at *number* instead of at 1.

`type="1|a|A|i|I "`
> Defines the numbering system for the list as follows:

Type value	Generated style	Sample sequence
1	Arabic numerals (default)	1, 2, 3, 4
A	Uppercase letters	A, B, C, D
a	Lowercase letters	a, b, c, d
I	Uppercase Roman numerals	I, II, III, IV
i	Lowercase Roman numerals	i, ii, iii, iv

Example

```
<ol>
  <li>Get out of bed</li>
  <li>Take a shower</li>
  <li>Walk the dog</li>
</ol>
```

---

optgroup

`<optgroup> . . . </optgroup>`

Defines a logical group of `option` elements within a `select` menu form control. An `optgroup` element may not contain other `optgroup` elements (they may not be nested).

Usage

Categories:
> None

Permitted contexts:
> As a child of a `select` element

Permitted content:
> Zero or more `option` elements

Start/end tags:
> Required/Optional (Required/Required in XHTML)

Attributes

HTML5 Global Attributes

`disabled` *(disabled="disabled" in XHTML)*
> Indicates that the group of options is nonfunctional. It can be reactivated with a script.

`label="text"`
> **Required**. Specifies the label for the option group.

Example

```
<p>What are your favorite ice cream flavors?<p>
<select name="ice_cream" size="6" multiple="multiple">
  <optgroup label="traditional">
    <option>Vanilla</option>
```

```
    <option>Chocolate</option>
  </optgroup>
  <optgroup label="specialty">
    <option>Inside-out Rocky Road</option>
    <option>Praline Pecan Smashup</option>
  </optgroup>
</select>
```

option

```
<option> . . . </option>
```

Defines an option within a select element (a multiple-choice menu or scrolling list) or a datalist element (a predefined list of text options for an input element). The content of the option element is the value that is sent to the form-processing application (unless an alternative value is specified using the value attribute).

Usage

Categories:
    None

Permitted contexts:
    As a child of a select, datalist, or optgroup element

Permitted content:
    Text

Start/end tags:
    Required/Optional (XHTML: Required/Required)

Attributes

HTML5 Global Attributes

disabled (disabled="disabled" *in XHTML*)
    Indicates that the selection is initially nonfunctional. It can be reactivated with a script.

label="*text*"
    Allows the author to provide a shorter label than the content of the option.

selected (selected="selected" *in XHTML*)
    Makes this item selected when the form is initially displayed.

value="*text*"
> Defines a value to assign to the option item within the select control to use in place of option contents.

Example

```
<p>What are your favorite ice cream flavors?</p>
<select name="ice_cream" size="4" multiple="multiple">
   <option>Vanilla</option>
   <option>Chocolate</option>
   <option>Inside-out Rocky Road</option>
   <option value="pecan">Praline Pecan Smashup</option>
   <option>Mint Chocolate Chip</option>
   <option>Pistachio</option>
</select>
```

output

`<output> . . . </output>`

Not in HTML 4.01. Represents the result of a calculation, most likely the output of a script.

Usage

Categories:
> Flow content, phrasing content, palpable content, and "listed, labelable and resettable form-associated content"

Permitted contexts:
> Where phrasing content is expected

Permitted content:
> Phrasing content

Start/end tags:
> Required/Required

Attributes

HTML5 Global Attributes

for="*text*"
> Creates an explicit relationship between the calculation result and a named element or elements on the page that are related to or influenced the calculation.

```
form="id of form owner"
```
Explicitly associates the input control with its associated form (its *form owner*). With this method, the output control does not need to be a child of the applicable form element.

```
name="text"
```
Gives an identifying name to the form control used in form submission.

Example

```
<form oninput="myCalc.value = parseInt(a.value) +
parseInt(b.value)">
<input type="number" id="a"> + <input type="number" id="b">
  = <output name="myCalc" for="a b">[displays value
  of a+b]</output>
</form>
```

---

p

```
<p> . . . </p>
```

Denotes a paragraph. Paragraphs may contain text and inline elements, but they may not contain other block elements, including other paragraphs. Browsers are instructed to ignore multiple empty p elements.

Usage

Categories:
Flow content, palpable content

Permitted contexts:
Where flow content is expected

Permitted content:
Phrasing content

Start/end tags:
Required/Optional (XHTML: Required/Required)

Attributes

HTML5 Global Attributes

Example

```
<p> Paragraphs are the most rudimentary elements of a text
document.</p>
<p>They are indicated by the <code>p</code> element.</p>
```

---

param

`<param>` (XHTML: `<param/>` or `<param />`)

Supplies a parameter within an object element. A parameter is info required by the media object at runtime.

Usage

Categories:
    None

Permitted contexts:
    As a child of an object element, before any flow content

Permitted content:
    Empty

Start/end tags:
    This is an empty (void) element, meaning it has only a start tag and may not have any contents. In HTML, the end tag is forbidden. In XHTML, the element must be closed with a trailing slash (`<param/>` or `<param />`).

Attributes

HTML5 Global Attributes

`name="text"`
    Required. Defines the name of the parameter.

`value="text"`
    Defines the value of the parameter.

Example

See also object.

```
<param name="autoStart" value="false">
```

---

pre

`<pre> . . . </pre>`

Delimits "preformatted" text, meaning that lines are displayed exactly as they are typed in, honoring whitespace such as multiple character spaces and line breaks. By default, text within a pre element is displayed in a monospace font so that spacing and alignment is preserved.

Usage

Categories:
    Flow content, palpable content

Permitted contexts:
    Where flow content is expected

Permitted content:
    Phrasing content

Start/end tags:
    Required/Required

Attributes

HTML5 Global Attributes

`xml:space="preserve"`
    XHTML only. Instructs XML processors to preserve the whitespace in the element.

Example

```
<pre>
This is                 an              example of

        text with a         lot of
                            curious
                            whitespace.
</pre>
```

progress

```
<progress> . . . </progress>
```

Not in HTML 4.01. Represents the completion progress of a task, such as downloading. The value measuring task completion can be provided by a script and inserted as content of the progress element or be provided with the value attribute. The progress element may be used even if the maximum value is not known, for example, to indicate a task waiting for a remote host to respond.

Usage

Categories:
Flow content, phrasing content, labelable element, palpable content

Permitted contexts:
Where phrasing content is expected

Permitted content:
Phrasing content, but may not contain progress elements

Start/end tags:
Required/Required

Attributes

HTML5 Global Attributes

max="*number*"
Indicates a measure of the total work the task requires. The default is 1.

value="*number*"
Specifies how much of the task has been completed.

Example

```
<p>Percent downloaded: <progress max="100"><span
id="completed">0</span>%</progress></p>
```

q

`<q> . . . </q>`

Delimits a short quotation that can be included inline, such as "to be or not to be." It differs from blockquote, which is a block-level element used for longer quotations. According to the specification, the user agent should automatically insert quotation marks before and after a quote element. When used with the lang (language) attribute, the browser may insert language-specific quotation marks.

Usage

Categories:
    Flow content, phrasing content, palpable content

Permitted contexts:
    Where phrasing content is expected

Permitted content:
    Phrasing content

Start/end tags:
    Required/Required

Attributes

HTML5 Global Attributes

`cite="URL"`
    Designates the source document from which the quotation was taken.

Example

```
<p>In that famous speech beginning, <q>Four score and
seven years ago,</q> ... </p>
```

rp

`<rp> . . . </rp>`

Not in HTML 4.01. Used within the ruby element to provide parentheses around ruby text to be shown by user agents that don't support ruby annotations.

Usage

Categories:
> None

Permitted contexts:
> As a child of a ruby element, either immediately before or immediately after an rt element

Permitted content:
> Phrasing content

Start/end tags:
> Required/Required

Attributes

HTML5 Global Attributes

Example

See also ruby.

In the following example, a browser that cannot display ruby annotation would display the rt content in parentheses after the ideograph:

```
<ruby>
汉 <rp>(</rp><rt>hàn</rt><rp>)</rp>
字 <rp>(</rp><rt>zì</rt><rp>)</rp>
</ruby>
```

The example shown for the rp, rt, and ruby elements was taken from the HTML5 Working Draft at whatwg.com, used with permission under an MIT License.

---

rt

`<rt> . . . </rt>`

Not in HTML 4.01. Used within the ruby element, rt provides the ruby text in ruby annotations. The hints typically render smaller near the original ideograph.

Usage

Categories:
None

Permitted contexts:
As the child of a ruby element

Permitted content:
Phrasing content

Start/end tags:
Required/Required

Attributes

HTML5 Global Attributes

Example

```
<ruby>
汉 <rt>hàn</rt>
字 <rt>zì</rt>
</ruby>
```

---

ruby

`<ruby> . . . </ruby>`

Not in HTML 4.01. Represents a run of text marked with *ruby annotations*, short guides to pronunciation, and other notes used primarily in East Asian typography.

Usage

Categories:
Flow content, phrasing content, palpable content

Permitted contexts:
Where phrasing content is expected

Permitted content:
Phrasing content, but may not contain ruby elements. May also contain one or more rt elements, optionally with rp elements before and after the rt element.

Start/end tags:
  Required/Required

Attributes

HTML5 Global Attributes

Example

In the following example, the pronunciation tips in the `rt` elements will be displayed above the ideographs in visual browsers:

```html
<ruby>
汉 <rt>hàn</rt>
字 <rt>zì</rt>
</ruby>
```

S

```html
<s> . . . </s>
```

Represents content that is no longer accurate or relevant. It is generally displayed as strikethrough text.

Usage

Categories:
  Flow content, phrasing content, palpable content

Permitted contexts:
  Where phrasing content is expected

Permitted content:
  Phrasing content

Start/end tags:
  Required/Required

Attributes

HTML5 Global Attributes

Example

```html
<p>All winter gear is <s>20%</s> 40% off.</p>
```

---

samp

```
<samp> . . . </samp>
```

Indicates sample output from programs, scripts, and so on.

Usage

Categories:
Flow content, phrasing content, palpable content

Permitted contexts:
Where phrasing content is expected

Permitted content:
Phrasing content

Start/end tags:
Required/Required

Attributes

HTML5 Global Attributes

Example

```
<p>Provide alternative error messages to <samp>404 Not
Found</samp>.</p>
```

script

```
<script> . . . </script>
```

Places a script in the document (usually JavaScript for web documents). It may appear any number of times in the head or body of the document. The script may be provided in the script element or in an external file (by providing the src attribute).

Notes

In XHTML, when the script is provided as the content of the script element (i.e., not as an external file), the script should be contained in a CDATA section, as shown in the example below.

Usage

Categories:
Metadata content, flow content, phrasing content

Permitted contexts:
Where metadata or phrasing content is expected

Permitted content:
If there is no `src` attribute, the content model depends on the `type` attribute. If there is a `src` attribute, the element must be either empty or contain only script documentation.

Start/end tags:
Required/Required

Attributes

HTML5 Global Attributes

`async` *(async="async" in XHTML)*
Not in HTML 4.01. Indicates an external script should be executed asynchronously, as soon as it is available.

`charset="character set"`
Indicates the character encoding of an external script document (it is not relevant to the content of the `script` element).

`crossorigin="anonymous|use-credentials"`
Not in HTML 4.01. For sites that allow scripts from other domains, this attribute determines whether error information for scripts from other origins will be exposed.

`defer` *(defer="defer" in XHTML)*
Indicates to the user agent that an external script should be executed once the page is finished parsing.

`src="URL"`
Provides the location of an external script.

`type="content-type"`
Required in HTML 4.01. Optional in HTML5 if using JavaScript. Specifies the scripting language used for the current script. The value is a content type, most often `text/javascript`.

xml:space="preserve"

> **XHTML only**. Instructs XML processors to preserve the
> whitespace in the element.

Examples

```
<script>
  var foo = 52;
  alert(foo);
<script>
```

```
<script src="my_script.js"><script>
```

Example (HTML 4.01)

```
<script type="text/javascript">
  // JavaScript code goes here
</script>
```

Example (XHTML)

```
<script>
  // <![CDATA[
    // JavaScript code goes here
  // ]]>
</script>
```

---

section

`<section> . . . </section>`

Not in HTML 4.01. Represents a section (a thematic grouping of
content) of a document or application with its own internal outline
and (optionally) a header and footer. The section element is not a
generic container; it should be used only if the element's contents
should appear in the document's outline.

Usage

Categories:
> Flow content, sectioning content, palpable content

Permitted contexts:
> Where flow content is expected

Permitted content:
    Flow content

Start/end tags:
    Required/Required

Attributes

HTML5 Global Attributes

Example

```
<body>
<article>
  <h1>Common Birds</h1>
  <section>
    <h1>Chapter 1: Hummingbirds</h1>
    <p>A little something on hummingbirds.</p>
  </section>
  <section>
    <h1>Chapter 2: Turkeys</h1>
    <p>This is about turkeys</p>
  </section>
</article>
</body>
```

select

`<select> . . . </select>`

Defines a multiple-choice menu or a scrolling list. It is a container for one or more option or optgroup elements.

Usage

Categories:
    Flow content, phrasing content, interactive content, palpable content, and "listed, labelable, submittable, and resettable form-associated element"

Permitted contexts:
    Where phrasing content is expected

Permitted content:
    Zero or more option or optgroup elements

Start/end tags:
> Required/Required

Attributes

HTML5 Global Attributes

`autofocus` (`autofocus="autofocus"` *in XHTML*)
> **Not in HTML 4.01**. Indicates the control should have focus (be highlighted and ready for user input) when the document loads.

`disabled` (`disabled="disabled"` *in XHTML*)
> Indicates that the `select` element is initially nonfunctional. It can be reactivated with a script.

`form="`*id of the form owner*`"`
> **Not in HTML 4.01**. Explicitly associates the `select` control with its associated form (its *form owner*). With this method, the control does not need to be a child of the `form` element that applies to it.

`inputmode="verbatim|latin|latin-name|latin-prose|`
`full-width-latin|kana|katakana|numeric|tel|email|url"`
> **Not in HTML 4.01**. Indicates what kind of input mechanism would be most helpful for users entering content into the form control. Applies to the `text` and `search` input types.

`multiple` (`multiple="multiple"` *in XHTML*)
> Allows the user to select more than one `option` from the list. When this attribute is absent, only single selections are allowed.

`name="`*text*`"`
> **Required**. Defines the name for the `select` control. When the form is submitted to the form-processing application, this name is sent along with each selected `option` value.

`required` (`required="required"` *in XHTML*)
> **Not in HTML 4.01**. When present, the user must select an option before the form can be submitted.

```
size="number"
```
Specifies the number of rows that display in the list of options. For values higher than 1, the options are displayed as a scrolling list with the specified number of options visible. When `size="1"` is specified, the list is displayed as a pop-up menu.

Example

```
<p>What are your favorite ice cream flavors?</p>
<select name="ice_cream" multiple="multiple">
  <option>Vanilla</option>
  <option>Chocolate</option>
  <option>Mint Chocolate Chip</option>
  <option>Pistachio</option>
</select>
```

---

small

```
<small> . . . </small>
```

Indicates an addendum or side note to the main text such as legal "small print" at the bottom of the document.

Usage

Categories:
Flow content, phrasing content, palpable content

Permitted contexts:
Where phrasing content is expected

Permitted content:
Phrasing content

Start/end tags:
Required/Required

Attributes

HTML5 Global Attributes

Example

```
<p><small>Copyright 2013, O'Reilly Media</small></p>
```

source

`<source>` (XHTML: `<source/>` or `<source />`)

Not in HTML 4.01. Used within `audio` and `video` elements, source allows authors to specify multiple versions of a media file. When source is used, the `src` attribute should be omitted from the `audio` and `video` elements. A user agent will go down the list of source elements until it finds a format it is able to play.

Usage

Categories:
> None

Permitted contexts:
> As the child of an `audio` or `video` element, before any flow content or `track` elements

Permitted content:
> Empty

Start/end tags:
> This is an empty (void) element, meaning it has only a start tag and may not have any contents. In HTML, the end tag is forbidden. In XHTML, the element must be closed with a trailing slash (`<source/>` or `<source />`).

Attributes

HTML5 Global Attributes

`media="all|aural|braille|handheld|print|projection|screen| tty|tv"`
> Specifies the target display media for the audio or video file

`src="URL"`
> Specifies the location of the audio or video file

`type="MIME type"`
> Indicates the file type of the media file and may also include the `codecs=` MIME parameter indicating the codec used to encode the media

Example

```
<video>
  <source src="media/vacation.ogv" type="video/ogg;
  codecs='theora, vorbis'">
  <source src="media/vacation.mp4" type="video/mp4">
  Your browser doesn't support the <code>video</code>
  element.
</video>
```

---

span

```
<span> . . . </span>
```

Identifies a generic inline element. The span element is typically given meaning with the class or id attributes, which also allow it to be accessible to scripts and selected in stylesheets.

Usage

Categories:
　　Flow content, phrasing content, palpable content

Permitted contexts:
　　Where phrasing content is expected

Permitted content:
　　Phrasing content

Start/end tags:
　　Required/Required

Attributes

HTML5 Global Attributes

Example

```
<li>Jenny: <span class="tel">867.5309</span></li>
```

strong

`<strong>` . . . `</strong>`

Indicates a word or phrase as important or requiring extra attention (typically displayed as bold text).

Usage

Categories:
  Flow content, phrasing content, palpable content

Permitted contexts:
  Where phrasing content is expected

Permitted content:
  Phrasing content

Start/end tags:
  Required/Required

Attributes

HTML5 Global Attributes

Example

```
<p>All applications are due <strong>no later than
February 14</strong>.</p>
```

style

`<style>` . . . `</style>`

Inserts one or more style rules (commonly Cascading Style Sheets) into the document. The style element should not be confused with the global style attribute for applying styles to an individual element.

Notes

In HTML5, the style element may be used in the content of the document. In HTML 4.01, it must appear in the head of a document.

Usage

Categories:
> Metadata content, flow content (if the `scoped` attribute is present)

Permitted contexts:
> Where metadata is expected or in a `noscript` element that is the child of a `head` element. If the `scoped` attribute is present, where flow content is expected, but before any other flow content other than interelement whitespace and not as the child of an element whose content model is transparent.

Permitted content:
> Style rules, dependent on the value of the `type` attribute. HTML5 assumes the styling language to be in CSS syntax.

Start/end tags:
> Required/Required

Attributes

HTML5 Global Attributes

`media="all|aural|braille|handheld|print|projection|screen|tty|tv"`
> Specifies the intended destination medium for the style information. It may be a single keyword or a comma-separated list. The default in the HTML 4.01 spec is `screen`. In HTML5, the default is `all`.

`scoped` (`scoped="scoped"` *in XHTML*)
> **Not in HTML 4.01**. Applies the styles only to the local document tree (i.e., only the descendants of the parent of the `style` element) rather than the whole document.

`type="content type"` (`text/css`)
> **Required in HTML 4.01 only**. Specifies the stylesheet language. For Cascading Style Sheets (currently the only style type option), the value is `text/css`. In HTML5, the `type` attribute is optional if using CSS.

`xml:space="preserve"`
> **XHTML only**. Instructs XML processors to preserve the whitespace in the element.

Example (HTML5 and CSS)

```
<head>
  <style>
    h1 {color: #666;}
    p {line-height: 2;}
  </style>
  <title>Scientific Presentation</title>
</head>
```

Example (HTML 4.01 and CSS)

```
<head>
  <style type="text/css">
    h1 {color: #666;}
    p {line-height: 2;}
  </style>
  <title>Scientific Presentation</title>
</head>
```

---

sub

```
<sub> . . . </sub>
```

Formats enclosed text as subscript. This element should be used only when subscript has a specific meaning, not for typographic effects.

Usage

Categories:
Flow content, phrasing content, palpable content

Permitted contexts:
Where phrasing content is expected

Permitted content:
Phrasing content

Start/end tags:
Required/Required

Attributes

HTML5 Global Attributes

Example

```
<p>H<sub>2</sub>0</p>
```

---

summary

```
<summary> . . . </summary>
```

Not in HTML 4.01. Provides a summary, caption, or legend for its parent details element.

Usage

Categories:
    None

Permitted contexts:
    As the first child of a details element

Permitted content:
    Phrasing content

Start/end tags:
    Required/Required

Attributes

HTML5 Global Attributes

Example

See also details.

```
<img src="lilyphoto.jpg" alt="Lily from Missouri Botanical
Gardens">
<details>
  <summary>More about this photo</summary>
  <p>This photo is of a daylily taken at the ....</p>
</details>
```

sup

`<sup> . . . </sup>`

Formats enclosed text as superscript. It should be used only when the superscript has specific meaning, not merely for typographic effect.

Usage

Categories:
    Flow content, phrasing content, palpable content

Permitted contexts:
    Where phrasing content is expected

Permitted content:
    Phrasing content

Start/end tags:
    Required/Required

Attributes

HTML5 Global Attributes

Example

```
<p>E=MC<sup>2</sup></p>
```

table

`<table> . . . </table>`

Indicates a table used for displaying rows and columns of data or information. The minimum elements for defining a table are table for establishing the table itself, tr for declaring a table row, and td for creating table cells within the row. The complete table model is shown below.

Usage

Categories:
    Flow content, palpable content

Permitted contexts:
> Where flow content is expected

Permitted content:
> In this order: optional `caption` element, then zero or more `colgroup` elements, followed optionally by a `thead` element, followed optionally by a `tfoot` element, followed by either zero or more `tbody` elements or one or more `tr` elements, followed optionally by a `tfoot` element (there may only be one `tfoot` element total)

Start/end tags:
> Required/Required

Attributes

HTML5 Global Attributes

`border="`*number of pixels*`"`
> **W3C only**. Specifies the width (in pixels) of the border around the table and its cells. Setting its value to 0 (zero) turns the borders off completely. The default value is 1. Adding the word `border` without a value results in a 1-pixel border, although this is not valid in XHTML.

`sortable` *(*`sortable="sortable"` *in XHTML)*
> **WHATWG & HTML5.1 only**. When present, it indicates the table's contents may be sorted by column. It is used in conjunction with the `sorted` attribute on the `th` element, which can be set manually or by the user agent when the user clicks a column.

Examples

A simple table with two rows (two `tr` elements) and three columns (three `td` elements in each `tr`):

```
<table>
  <tr>
    <td>cell 1</td>
    <td>cell 2</td>
    <td>cell 3</td>
  </tr>
  <tr>
    <td>cell 4</td>
    <td>cell 5</td>
```

```
        <td>cell 6</td>
      </tr>
    </table>
```

The proper element order in the full table model (for details, see the caption, tbody, thead, tfoot, colgroup, and col element entries):

```
    <table>
      <caption>Employee salaries and start dates</caption>
      <colgroup id="employeeinfo">
        <col span="2">
        <col span="1">
      </colgroup>
    <thead>
      <tr>
        <th>Employee</th><th>Salary</th><th>Start date</th>
      </tr>
    </thead>
    <tfoot>
      <tr>
        <td colspan="3">Compiled by Betty D. Boss</td>
      </tr>
    </tfoot>
    <tbody>
      <tr>
        <td>Wilma</td><td>50,000</td><td>April 6</td>
      </tr>
      <tr>...more data cells...</tr>
      <tr>...more data cells...</tr>
    </tbody>
    </table>
```

tbody

`<tbody> . . . </tbody>`

Defines a row or group of rows as the "body" of the table. It must contain at least one row element (tr). "Row group" elements (tbody, thead, and tfoot) could speed table display and provide a mechanism for scrolling the body of a table independently of its head and foot, or repeat the head and foot when a long table is printed across several pages.

Usage

Categories:
None

Permitted contexts:
As the child of a table element, after any caption, colgroup, and thead elements, but only if there are no tr elements that are children of the table element

Permitted content:
Zero or more tr elements

Start/end tags:
HTML: Start tag is optional if first element in the table is a tr and not preceded by tbody, thead, tfoot, or an end tag. End tag optional if immediately followed by tbody or tfoot if there is no more content in the parent table; XHTML: Required/Required

Attributes

HTML5 Global Attributes

Example

See table.

---

td

`<td> . . . </td>`

Defines a table data cell. A table cell may contain any content, including another table.

Usage

Categories:
Sectioning root

Permitted contexts:
As the child of a tr element

Permitted content:
Flow content

Start/end tags:

HTML: Start tag required. End tag is optional if followed by `<td>` or `<th>` or end tag of parent element; XHTML: Required/Required

Attributes

HTML5 Global Attributes

`colspan="`*number*`"`

Specifies the number of columns the current cell should span. The default value is 1.

`headers="`*id reference*`"`

Lists header cells (by `id` value) that provide header information for the current data cell. This is intended to make tables more accessible to nonvisual browsers.

`rowspan="`*number*`"`

Specifies the number of rows spanned by the current cell. The default value is 1.

Example

```
<table>
  <tr>
    <td colspan="2">Cell 1</td>
  </tr>
  <tr>
    <td>Cell 3</td><td>Cell 4</td>
  </tr>
</table>
```

---

textarea

`<textarea> . . . </textarea>`

Defines a multiline text entry control. The content of the `textarea` element is displayed in the text entry field when the form initially displays and will be sent to the server. It is common for developers to put nothing in the `textarea` element and use the `placeholder` or `title` attributes to provide a hint of what to write instead.

Usage

Categories:
> Flow content, phrasing content, interactive content, palpable content, and "listed, labelable, submittable and resettable form-associated element"

Permitted contexts:
> Where phrasing content is expected

Permitted content:
> Text

Start/end tags:
> Required/Required

Attributes

HTML5 Global Attributes

autocomplete="on|off"
> **Not in HTML 4.01**. Allows the user agent (browser) to fill in a field automatically (on) or requires the user to enter the information every time (off). Omitting this attribute causes the control to inherit the autocomplete setting for the associated form element.

autofocus (autofocus="autofocus" *in XHTML*)
> **Not in HTML 4.01**. Indicates the control should have focus (be highlighted and ready for user input) when the document loads.

cols="*number*"
> Specifies the expected maximum number of characters per line. Visual browsers wrap the user's input so each line is less than the cols value. If wrap is set to hard, then the cols attribute is required.

dirname="*name of input field*"
> **Not in HTML 4.01**. Specifies the name of an input field that has text direction (ltr or rtl) instructions for the textarea.

disabled (disabled="disabled" *in XHTML*)
> Disables the control for user input. It can be altered only via a script. Browsers may display disabled controls differently

(grayed out, for example), which could be useful for dimming certain controls until required info is supplied.

`form="id of form owner"`
Not in HTML 4.01. Explicitly associates the `textarea` control with its associated form (its *form owner*). With this method, the `textarea` does not need to be a child of the `form` element that applies to it.

`inputmode="verbatim|latin|latin-name|latin-prose|`
`full-width-latin|kana|katakana|numeric|tel|email|url"`
Not in HTML 4.01. Indicates what kind of input mechanism would be most helpful for users entering content into the form control. Applies to the `text` and `search` input types.

`maxlength="number"`
Not in HTML 4.01. Specifies the maximum number of characters the user can input for the `textarea` element.

`name="text"`
Required. Specifies a name for the control. This name will be sent along with the control content to the form-processing application.

`placeholder="text"`
Not in HTML 4.01. Provides a short (one word or short phrase) hint or example to help the user enter the correct data. If a longer description is necessary, use the `title` attribute.

`readonly (readonly="readonly" in XHTML)`
Indicates that the form control may not be modified.

`required (required="required" in XHTML)`
Not in HTML 4.01. When present, indicates the user must enter a value in the control before submitting the form.

`rows="number"`
Specifies the height of the text entry field in number of lines of text. If the user enters more lines than are visible, the text field scrolls down to accommodate the extra lines.

`wrap="hard|soft"`
Not in HTML 4.01. When set to `hard`, hard returns (carriage return + line feed characters) are inserted at the end of lines as they appear in text entry field. When set to `hard`, there must

also be a `cols` attribute specifying the length of the line. When set to `soft` (the default), line breaks in the text entry field are not preserved in the returned data.

Examples

```
<p><label for="loveband">Official Contest Entry</label></p>
<textarea name="band" id="loveband" rows="4" cols="45">Tell
us why you love the band.</textarea>
```

```
<p><label for="loveband">Official Contest Entry</label></p>
<textarea name="band" id="loveband" rows="4" cols="45"
placeholder="Tell us why you love the band."></textarea>
```

---

tfoot

`<tfoot>` . . . `</tfoot>`

Defines a table footer. It is one of the "row group" elements. The tfoot element must appear after any caption, colgroup, and thead elements. It may appear before or after the tbody element. There may only be one tfoot element in a table.

Usage

Categories:
> None

Permitted contexts:
> As a child of a table element, after any caption, colgroup, and thead elements and before any tbody and tr elements, but only if there are no other tfoot elements in the parent table element. As a child of a table element, after any caption, colgroup, thead, tbody, and tr elements but only if there are no other tfoot elements in the parent table element.

Permitted content:
> Zero or more tr elements

Start/end tags:
> HTML: Start tag is required. End tag is optional if followed by a tbody or if there is no more content in the parent element; XHTML: Required/Required

---

Attributes

HTML5 Global Attributes

Example

See `table`.

---

th

`<th> . . . </th>`

Defines a table header cell. Table header cells provide important information and context to the table cells in the row or column that they precede. They are important for making the information in tables accessible. In terms of markup, they function the same as table data cells (`td`).

Usage

Categories:
> None, unless the `th` has the `sorted` attribute and is a sorting interface, then interactive content

Permitted contexts:
> As the child of a `tr` element

Permitted content:
> Flow content, but may not contain `header`, `footer`, sectioning content, or heading content. If the `th` element is a sorting interface, then it must not contain any interactive content.

Start/end tags:
> HTML: Required/Optional (if followed by a `td` or `th` or if the parent element ends); XHTML: Required/Required

Attributes

HTML5 Global Attributes

`colspan="number"`
> Specifies the number of columns the current cell should span. The default value is 1.

`headers="`*`id reference`*`"`

> Lists header cells (by id value) that provide header information for the current data cell. This is intended to make tables more accessible to nonvisual browsers.

`rowspan="`*`number`*`"`

> Specifies the number of rows spanned by the current cell. The default value is 1.

`scope="row|col|rowgroup|colgroup"`

> Indicates to which group of cells the header applies. For example, if scope=row, then the header cell applies the subsequent cells in the same row.

`sorted="reversed|number greater than zero"` *or both in any order*

> **WHATWG and HTML5.1 only**. Provides a means for users to sort table columns in tables with the sortable attribute.

Example

```
<table>
<tr><th>Planet</th><th>Distance from Earth</th></tr>
<tr><td>Venus</td><td>pretty darn far</td></tr>
<tr><td>Neptune</td><td>ridiculously far</td></tr>
</table>
```

thead

`<thead> . . . </thead>`

Defines a block of rows that consist of the column labels (headers) for the table. The thead element is one of the "row group" elements. It may be used to duplicate headers when the full table is broken over pages or for a static header that appears with a scrolling table body. It must contain at least one row (tr) with th or td elements.

Usage

Categories:

> None

Permitted contexts:

> As a child of a table element, after any caption and colgroup elements and before any tbody, tfoot, and tr elements, but

only if there are no other `thead` elements in the parent `table` element

Permitted content:
Zero or more `tr` elements

Start/end tags:
HTML: Optional/Optional (if followed by `tbody` or `tfoot`); XHTML: Required/Required

Attributes

HTML5 Global Attributes

Example

See `table`.

---

time

```
<time> . . . </time>
```

Not in HTML 4.01. Represents a time on a 24-hour clock or a date on the Gregorian calendar, optionally with time and a time zone offset. The `time` element could be used to pass time and date information in a machine-readable manner to other applications (e.g., saving an event to a personal calendar) or to restyle time information into alternate formats (e.g., 18:00 to 6 p.m.). The `time` element is not intended to be used to mark up times for which a precise time or date cannot be established, such as "the end of last year" or "the turn of the century."

Usage

Categories:
Flow content, phrasing content, palpable content

Permitted contexts:
Where phrasing content is expected

Permitted content:
Phrasing content

Start/end tags:
Required/Required

Attributes

HTML5 Global Attributes

pubdate *(pubdate="pubdate" in XHTML)*
> **W3C only (not in WHATWG)**. Indicates that the date and time provided by datetime is the publication date and time of the parent element (the article or whole document).

datetime="*YYYY-MM-DDThh:mm:ssTZD*"
> Identifies the date or time being specified. If the datetime attribute is used, the time element may be empty.

Examples

```
The deadline for entries is <time datetime="2013-02-15T
20:00-05:00">February 15, 2013, 8pm EST</time>

Hours: <time>8am</time> to <time>9pm</time>
```

---

title

```
<title> . . . </title>
```

Required. Specifies the title of the document. All documents must contain a meaningful title within the head of the document. Titles should contain only ASCII characters (letters, numbers, and basic punctuation). Special characters (such as &) should be referred to by their character entities within the title.

Titles should be clear and descriptive. The title is typically displayed in the top bar of the browser, outside the regular content window, as well as in a user's bookmarks or favorites list. Search engines also rely heavily on document titles.

Usage

Categories:
> Metadata content

Permitted contexts:
> In a head element. There may be no more than one title element and it may not contain other elements.

Permitted content:
    Text

Start/end tags:
    Required/Required

Attributes

HTML5 Global Attributes

Example

```
<head>
  <title>White Rabbits: Milk Famous</title>
</head>
```

---

tr

```
<tr> . . . </tr>
```

Defines a row of cells within a table. A tr element may contain only some number of td and/or th elements. It may be used only within a table, thead, tfoot, or tbody element.

Usage

Categories:
    None

Permitted contexts:
    As the child of a thead, tbody, or tfoot element. As the child of a table element, after any caption, colgroup, and thead elements, but only if there are no tbody elements.

Permitted content:
    Zero or more tr or th elements

Start/end tags:
    HTML: Required/Optional (if followed by another tr or the end of the parent element); XHTML: Required/Required

Attributes

HTML5 Global Attributes

Example

```
<table>
  <tr>
    <td>cell 1</td><td>cell 2</td>
  </tr>
  <tr>
    <td>cell 3</td><td>cell 4</td>
  </tr>
</table>
```

---

track

`<track>` (XHTML: `<track/>` or `<track />`)

Not in HTML 4.01. Specifies an external resource (text or audio) that is timed with a video or audio media file that improves accessibility or enhances navigation.

Usage

Categories:
   None

Permitted contexts:
   As a child of an audio or video element, before any flow content

Permitted content:
   Empty

Start/end tags:
   This is an empty (void) element, meaning it has only a start tag and may not have any contents. In HTML, the end tag is forbidden. In XHTML, the element must be closed with a trailing slash (`<track/>` or `<track />`).

Attributes

HTML5 Global Attributes

`default` (default="default" *in XHTML*)
   Indicates that the track should be used by default if it does not override user preferences.

`kind="subtitles|captions|descriptions|chapters|metadata"`

Indicates the intended purpose of the external track resource. subtitles provide a transcription or translation of dialogue that display over a video; captions provide a complete description of the audio (including sound effects and other audio cues) for when audio is not available or for the hard-of-hearing; descriptions indicates the resource is an audio track that describes what is happening in a video when it cannot be viewed; chapters are chapter titles used for navigating the media resource; and metadata is a track intended to be used by scripts but are not displayed. The default is subtitles.

`label="text string"`

Provides a title for the track that may be displayed by the browser.

`src="URL"`

Required. Provides the location of the text track data.

`srclang="2-letter language code"`

Required for subtitles. Specifies the language of the text track data.

Example

```
<video src="blockbuster.webm">
  <track kind="subtitles" src="blockbuster.en.vtt"
      srclang="en" label="English">
  <track kind="subtitles" src="blockbuster.de.vtt"
      srclang="de" label="Deutsch">
</video>
```

---

u

`<u> . . . </u>`

Enclosed text is underlined for semantic purposes, such as keywords or to indicate misspelt words in a spellcheck. Underlined text is easily confused as a link and should generally be avoided except for a few niche cases. Use other markup elements or CSS properties to indicate phrases that require special attention.

Usage

Categories:
Flow content, phrasing content, palpable content

Permitted contexts:
Where phrasing content is expected

Permitted content:
Phrasing content

Start/end tags:
Required/Required

Attributes

HTML5 Global Attributes

Example

```
<p><u>Underlined</u> text may be mistaken for a link.</p>
```

---

ul

```
<ul> . . . </ul>
```

Defines an unordered list, in which the order of the list items (li) is not important. By default, visual browsers display items in an unordered list with bullets. Lists may be formatted in any fashion (including as horizontal navigation elements) using Cascading Style Sheet properties.

Usage

Categories:
Flow content; if it contains at least one li element, then palpable content

Permitted contexts:
Where flow content is expected

Permitted content:
Zero or more li elements

Start/end tags:
Required/Required

Attributes

HTML5 Global Attributes

Example

```
<ul>
  <li>About</li>
  <li>Portfolio</li>
  <li>Blog</li>
  <li>Contact</li>
</ul>
```

---

var

`<var> . . . </var>`

Indicates an instance of a variable or program argument.

Usage

Categories:
    Flow content, phrasing content, palpable content

Permitted contexts:
    Where phrasing content is expected

Permitted content:
    Phrasing content

Start/end tags:
    Required/Required

Attributes

HTML5 Global Attributes

Example

```
<code><var>myString</var> = 'hello world';</code>
```

video

```
<video> . . . </video>
```

Not in HTML 4.01. Embeds a video file in the web page. The video resource can be provided with the src attribute or by one or more source elements inside the video element to provide several video format options. Other fallback content may be provided in the video element to display by agents that don't support the video element.

Notes

There is still debate regarding the supported video formats for the video element. No file format is supported by all browsers. As of this writing, browser support for available file formats is as follows:

IE 9+ (versions prior to 9 do not support the video element): MP4/H.264 (MIME type needs to be set correctly on the server for video to play), and WebM (by installing components from The WebM project at *www.webm-project.org*).

Chrome 5+: MP4 (H.264 + AAC), Ogg Theora/Vorbis, and WebM (6+)

Firefox 3.5+: Ogg Theora/Vorbis, and WebM (4+)

Safari 4+ and Mobile Safari 3+: MP4 (H.264 + AAC)

Android (2.1+): MP4 (H.264 + AAC), and WebM (2.3.3+)

Usage

Categories:
Flow content, phrasing content, embedded content, interactive content (if it has a controls attribute), palpable content

Permitted contexts:
Where embedded content is expected

Permitted content:
If it has a src attribute, then zero or more track elements, then transparent but with no audio or video element descendants. If it does not have a src attribute, then zero or more source elements, then zero or more track elements, then transparent but with no audio or video descendants.

Start/end tags:
    Required/Required

Attributes

HTML5 Global Attributes

autoplay *(autoplay="autoplay" in XHTML)*
    Makes the media file start playing automatically.

controls *(controls="controls" in XHTML)*
    Indicates that the user agent (browser) should display a set of playback controls for the media file, generally a play/pause button, a "seeker" that lets you move to a position within the video, and volume controls.

crossorigin="anonymous|use-credentials"
    Indicates if the user agent must check for credentials for a media file that is coming from a URL with a different origin than the source document. The default is anonymous (no credentials needed).

height="*number*"
    Specifies the height of the video player in pixels.

loop *(loop="loop" in XHTML)*
    Indicates that the media file should start playing again from the beginning once it reaches the end.

mediagroup ="*text*"
    Links multiple media elements together by assigning them the same mediagroup value.

muted *(or muted="muted" in XHTML)*
    Disables (mutes) the audio output, even if it overrides user preferences.

poster="*URL*"
    Specifies the location of an image file that displays as a placeholder before the video begins to play.

`preload="none|metadata|auto"`

> Hints to the browser whether the media file should begin to load automatically based on anticipated best user experience. none prevents the preload; metadata does not download the media file, but does fetch the resource metadata; and auto leaves the decision to preload to the user agent.

`src="URL"`

> Specifies the location of the media file.

`width="number"`

> Specifies the width of the video player in pixels.

Examples

```
<video src="movies/nantucket.ogv" width="640" height="480"
  poster="bay.jpg" type="video/ogg; codecs='theora,
  vorbis'">
  This browser does not support the <code>video</code>
  element.</video>

<video id="yourmovieid" width="640" height="360"
poster="yourmovie_still.jpg" controls preload="auto">
  <source src="yourmovie-baseline.mp4" type='video/mp4;
codecs="avc1.42E01E, mp4a.40.2"'>
  <source src="yourmovie.ogv" type='video/ogg; codecs=
"theora, vorbis"'>
  <!--Flash fallback -->
  <object width="640" height="360" type="application/
x-shockwave-flash" data="your_flash_player.swf">
    <param name="movie" value="your_flash_player.swf">
    <param name="flashvars" value="controlbar=over&amp;
image=poster.jpg&amp;
        file=yourmovie-main.mp4">
    <img src="poster.jpg" width="640" height="360" alt=""
        title="No video playback capabilities, please
download the video below">
  </object>
</video>
<p>Download the Highlights Reel:</p>
<ul>
    <li><a href="yourmovie.mp4">MPEG-4 format</a></li>
    <li><a href="yourmovie.ogv">Ogg Theora format</a></li>
</ul>
```

wbr

`<wbr>` (XHTML: `<wbr/>` or `<wbr />`)

Not in HTML 4.01. Represents a line break opportunity within a word, allowing the author to instruct at which point a long word should optimally break. The line will only break at the location of the wbr element if it needs to.

Usage

Categories:
> Flow content, phrasing content

Permitted contexts:
> Where phrasing content is expected

Permitted content:
> Empty

Start/end tags:
> This is an empty (void) element, meaning it has only a start tag and may not have any contents. In HTML, the end tag is forbidden. In XHTML, the element must be closed with a trailing slash (`<wbr/>` or `<wbr />`).

Attributes

HTML5 Global Attributes

Example

```
<p>The biggest word you've ever heard & this is how it goes:
<em>supercali<wbr>fragilistic<wbr>expialidocious</em>!</p>
```

Elements Organized by Function

This section organizes the elements in HTML5 into groups related to concept or function. Elements that are new in HTML5 and were not part of the HTML 4.01 specification are indicated with (5).

Root Element

html

Metadata Elements

base, head, link, meta, title, style

Text: Sections

address, article (5), aside (5), body, footer (5), header (5), hr, main (5), nav (5), section (5)

Text: Headings

h1, h2, h3, h4, h5, h6, hgroup (5, removed from HTML5.1)

Text: Grouping Elements

See also **Text: lists**

blockquote, div, figcaption (5), figure (5), hr, main (5), p, pre

Text: Lists

dd, dl, dt, li, ol, ul

Text-Level (Inline) Elements

abbr, b, bdi (5), bdo, br, cite, code, del, dfn, em, i, ins, kbd, mark (5), q, s, samp, small (5), span, strong, sub, sup, time (5), u, var, wbr

Tables

caption, col, colgroup, table, tbody, td, tfoot, th, thead, tr

Form Elements

button, datalist (5), fieldset, form, input, keygen (5), label, legend, meter (5), optgroup, option, output (5), progress (5), select, textarea

Interactive Content

a, details (5), dialog (5), menu (5), menuitem (5), summary (5)

Embedded Content

area, audio (5), canvas (5), embed (5), iframe, img, map, object, param, source (5), track (5), video (5)

Scripting

script, noscript

Ruby Annotation

rp (5), rt (5), ruby (5)

Character Entities

Characters not found in the normal alphanumeric character set, such as < and &, may be specified in HTML and XHTML documents using character references. This process is known as *escaping* the character. Escaped characters are indicated by character references that begin with & and end with ;. The character may be referred to by its Numeric Character Reference (NCR) or a predefined character entity name.

A *Numeric Character Reference* refers to a character by its Unicode code point in either decimal or hexadecimal form. Hexadecimal values are indicated by an "x": &#xhhhh;. Decimal character references use the syntax &#nnnn; (no "x" character). For example, the em-dash (—) character has the Unicode code point U+02014, which can be identified as &#x2014 (hexadecimal) or — (decimal) in an HTML document.

Character entities (or *Named Character References*) are abbreviated names for characters, such as < for the less-than symbol. Character entities are predefined in markup languages such as HTML and XHTML as a convenience to authors because they may be easier to remember than Numeric Character References. HTML 4.01 defined 252 character entities. That number has grown to more than 2,000 in HTML5.

The remainder of this section lists only the most commonly used character references and entities. For additional character references, see the following resources:

W3C Character Entity Reference Chart (http://dev.w3.org/ html5/html-author/charref)
> This visual chart organizes 488 characters in numerical order by Unicode code point. It features extra large characters for easy scanning and lists both numeric and named references.

HTML5 Named Character Reference list (http://www.w3.org/ TR/2011/WD-html5-20110113/named-character-references .html)
> This definitive list of more than 2,000 references is organized alphabetically by entity name and includes Unicode code points only.

W3Schools.com HTML 4.01 Character Reference List (http:// www.w3schools.com/tags/ref_entities.asp)
> A complete list of entity numbers and names supported in HTML 4.01, including a complete ASCII reference, complete ISO-8859-1 reference, mathematical symbols, Greek letters, and other symbols.

XML Named Entities

In XHTML and other XML languages, the quote, ampersand, apostrophe, less-than, and greater-than symbols must always be escaped in the content and metadata of the document.

Decimal	Entity	Symbol	Description
"	"	"	Quotation mark
'	'	'	Apostrophe
&	&	&	Ampersand
<	<	<	Less-than
>	>	>	Greater-than

Latin-1 (ISO-8859-1)

Unicode	Decimal	Entity	Symbol	Description
U+00A0				Nonbreaking space
U+00A1	¡	¡	¡	Inverted exclamation mark
U+00A2	¢	¢	¢	Cent sign
U+00A3	£	£	£	Pound symbol
U+00A4	¤	¤	¤	General currency symbol
U+00A5	¥	¥	¥	Yen symbol
U+00A6	¦	¦	¦	Broken vertical bar
U+00A7	§	§	§	Section sign
U+00A8	¨	¨	¨	Umlaut
U+00A9	©	©	©	Copyright
U+00AA	ª	ª	ª	Feminine ordinal
U+00AB	«	«	«	Left angle quote
U+00AC	¬	¬	¬	Not sign
U+00AD	­	­	-	Soft hyphen
U+00AE	®	®	®	Registered trademark
U+00AF	¯	¯	¯	Macron accent
U+00B0	°	°	°	Degree sign
U+00B1	±	±	±	Plus or minus
U+00B2	²	²	²	Superscript 2
U+00B3	³	³	³	Superscript 3
U+00B4	´	´	´	Acute accent (no letter)
U+00B5	µ	µ	µ	Micron (Greek mu)
U+00B6	¶	¶	¶	Paragraph sign
U+00B7	·	·	·	Middle dot
U+00B8	¸	¸	¸	Cedilla
U+00B9	¹	¹	¹	Superscript 1
U+00BA	º	º	º	Masculine ordinal

Unicode	Decimal	Entity	Symbol	Description
U+000BB	»	»	»	Right angle quote
U+000BC	¼	¼	¼	Fraction one-fourth
U+000BD	½	½	½	Fraction one-half
U+000BE	¾	¾	¾	Fraction three-fourths
U+000BF	¿	¿	¿	Inverted question mark
U+000C0	À	À	À	Capital A, grave accent
U+000C1	Á	Á	Á	Capital A, acute accent
U+000C2	Â	Â	Â	Capital A, circumflex accent
U+000C3	Ã	Ã	Ã	Capital A, tilde accent
U+000C4	Ä	Ä	Ä	Capital A, umlaut
U+000C5	Å	&Aring	Å	Capital A, ring
U+000C6	Æ	Æ	Æ	Capital AE ligature
U+000C7	Ç	Ç	Ç	Capital C, cedilla
U+000C8	È	&Egrave	È	Capital E, grave accent
U+000C9	É	É	É	Capital E, acute accent
U+000CA	Ê	Ê	Ê	Capital E, circumflex accent
U+000CB	Ë	Ë	Ë	Capital E, umlaut
U+000CC	Ì	Ì	Ì	Capital I, grave accent
U+000CD	Í	Í	Í	Capital I, acute accent
U+000CE	Î	Î	Î	Capital I, circumflex accent
U+000CF	Ï	Ï	Ï	Capital I, umlaut
U+000D0	Ð	Ð	Ð	Capital eth, Icelandic
U+000D1	Ñ	Ñ	Ñ	Capital N, tilde
U+000D2	Ò	Ò	Ò	Capital O, grave accent
U+000D3	Ó	Ó	Ó	Capital O, acute accent
U+000D4	Ô	Ô	Ô	Capital O, circumflex accent
U+000D5	Õ	Õ	Õ	Capital O, tilde accent
U+000D6	Ö	Ö	Ö	Capital O, umlaut

Unicode	Decimal	Entity	Symbol	Description
U+000D7	×	×	×	Multiplication sign
U+000D8	Ø	Ø	Ø	Capital O, slash
U+000D9	Ù	Ù	Ù	Capital U, grave accent
U+000DA	Ú	Ú	Ú	Capital U, acute accent
U+000DB	Û	Û	Û	Capital U, circumflex accent
U+000DC	Ü	Ü	Ü	Capital U, umlaut
U+000DD	Ý	Ý	Ý	Capital Y, acute accent
U+000DE	Þ	Þ	Þ	Capital Thorn, Icelandic
U+000DF	ß	ß	ß	Small sz ligature, German
U+000E0	à	à	à	Small a, grave accent
U+000E1	á	á	á	Small a, acute accent
U+000E2	â	â	â	Small a, circumflex accent
U+000E3	ã	ã	ã	Small a, tilde
U+000E4	ä	ä	ä	Small a, umlaut
U+000E5	å	å	å	Small a, ring
U+000E6	æ	æ	æ	Small ae ligature
U+000E7	ç	ç	ç	Small c, cedilla
U+000E8	è	è	è	Small e, grave accent
U+000E9	é	é	é	Small e, acute accent
U+000EA	ê	ê	ê	Small e, circumflex accent
U+000EB	ë	ë	ë	Small e, umlaut
U+000EC	ì	ì	ì	Small i, grave accent
U+000ED	í	í	í	Small i, acute accent
U+000EE	î	î	î	Small i, circumflex accent
U+000EF	ï	ï	ï	Small i, umlaut
U+000F0	ð	ð	ð	Small eth, Icelandic
U+000F1	ñ	ñ	ñ	Small n, tilde
U+000F2	ò	ò	ò	Small o, grave accent

Unicode	Decimal	Entity	Symbol	Description
U+000F3	&#243;	&oacute;	ó	Small o, acute accent
U+000F4	&#244;	&ocirc;	ô	Small o, circumflex accent
U+000F5	&#245;	&otilde;	õ	Small o, tilde
U+000F6	&#246;	&ouml;	ö	Small o, umlaut
U+000F7	&#247;	&divide;	÷	Division sign
U+000F8	&#248;	&oslash;	ø	Small o, slash
U+000F9	&#249;	&ugrave;	ù	Small u, grave accent
U+000FA	&#250;	&uacute;	ú	Small u, acute accent
U+000FB	&#251;	&ucirc;	û	Small u, circumflex accent
U+000FC	&#252;	&uuml;	ü	Small u, umlaut
U+000FD	&#253;	&yacute;	ý	Small y, acute accent
U+000FE	&#254;	&thorn;	þ	Small thorn, Icelandic
U+000FF	&#255;	&yuml;	ÿ	Small y, umlaut

Spacing Modifier Letters

Unicode	Decimal	Entity	Symbol	Description
U+002C6	&#710;	&circ;	ˆ	Circumflex accent
U+002DC	&#732;	&tilde;	˜	Tilde

General Punctuation

Unicode	Decimal	Entity	Symbol	Description
U+02002				En space
U+02003				Em space
U+02009				Thin space
U+0200C	&#8204;	&zwnj;	Nonprinting	Zero-width nonjoiner
U+0200D	&#8205;	&zwj;	Nonprinting	Zero-width joiner
U+0200E	&#8206;	&lrm;	Nonprinting	Left-to-right mark

Unicode	Decimal	Entity	Symbol	Description
U+0200F	‏	‏	Nonprinting	Right-to-left mark
U+02013	–	–	-	En dash
U+02014	—	—	—	Em dash
U+02018	‘	‘	'	Left single quotation mark
U+02019	’	’	'	Right single quotation mark
U+0201A	‚	‚	,	Single low-9 quotation mark
U+0201C	“	“	"	Left double quotation mark
U+0201D	”	”	"	Right double quotation mark
U+0201E	„	„	„	Double low-9 quotation mark
U+02020	†	†	†	Dagger
U+02021	‡	‡	‡	Double dagger
U+02022	•	•	•	Bullet
U+02026	…	…	…	Ellipses
U+02030	‰	‰	‰	Per mille symbol (per thousand)
U+02032	′	′	′	Prime, minutes, feet
U+02033	″	″	″	Double prime, seconds, inches
U+02039	‹	‹	‹	Single left angle quotation
U+0203A	›	›	›	Single right angle quotation
U+0203E	‾	‾	‾	Overline
U+02044	⁄	⁄	/	Fraction slash
U+020AC	€	€	€	Euro symbol

NOTE

The mathematical symbols for "equivalent to" ($\equiv$, represented by ≡ or ≡) and "colon equals" ($:=$, represented by ≔ or ≔) are commonly used as symbols for navigation in mobile site development because of their resemblance to a list of options.

XHTML Syntax Overview

XHTML (eXtensible HyperText Markup Language) is a reformulation of HTML according to the stricter syntax rules of XML (eXtensible Markup Language). HTML5 can be written using XHTML syntax (formally called the XML Serialization of HTML5). This section describes the ways in which XHTML syntax differs from HTML.

Because XHTML is an XML language, its syntax is stricter and differs from HTML in these key ways:

- All element names and attributes must be lowercase. For example, `<a href="example.com">...</a>`.

- All elements must be terminated—that is, they must include an end tag. For example, `<p>...</p>`.

- Empty elements must be terminated as well. This is done by including a slash at the end of the tag. A space is commonly added before the slash for backward compatibility with older browsers—for example, `<hr />`, `<img />`, and `<meta />`.

- All attribute values must be contained in quotation marks (either single or double). For example, `<td colspan="2">`.

- All attribute values must be explicit and may not be minimized to one word, as is permitted in HTML—for example, `checked="checked"`.

- Nesting restrictions are more strictly enforced. These restrictions are explicitly stated:

  — An `a` element cannot contain another `a` element.

  — The `pre` element cannot contain `img`, `object`, `applet`, `big`, `small`, `sub`, `sup`, `font`, or `basefont`.

  — The `form` element may not contain other `form` elements.

  — A `button` element cannot contain `a`, `form`, `input`, `select`, `textarea`, `label`, `button`, `iframe`, or `isindex`.

  — The `label` element cannot contain other `label` elements.

- The special characters <, >, &, ', and " must always be represented by their character entities, including when they appear within attribute values. For example, `&lt;`, `&gt;`, `&amp;`, `&apos;`, and `&quot;` (respectively).

- XHTML documents must use `id` instead of `name` for identifying document fragments and in `a`, `applet`, `form`, `frame`, `iframe`, `img`, and `map` elements.

- XHTML documents should be served as XML applications, not as HTML text documents. More specifically, the server should be configured to serve XHTML documents with the Content-type header set to `application/xhtml+xml`. If it is not possible to configure the server, the content type may be specified in a `meta` element in the document's `head`, as shown in this example:

  ```
  <meta http-equiv="content-type"
    content="application/xhtml+xml; charset=UTF-8" />
  ```

Unfortunately, some popular browsers (Internet Explorer in particular) cannot parse XHTML documents as XML, causing pages to break. For more information on XHTML MIME types, see *www.w3.org/TR/xhtm-media-types/*.

Index

We'd like to hear your suggestions for improving our indexes. Send email to
index@oreilly.com.

Get even more for your money.

Join the O'Reilly Community, and register the O'Reilly books you own. It's free, and you'll get:

- $4.99 ebook upgrade offer
- 40% upgrade offer on O'Reilly print books
- Membership discounts on books and events
- Free lifetime updates to ebooks and videos
- Multiple ebook formats, DRM FREE
- Participation in the O'Reilly community
- Newsletters
- Account management
- 100% Satisfaction Guarantee

Registering your books is easy:

1. Go to: oreilly.com/go/register
2. Create an O'Reilly login.
3. Provide your address.
4. Register your books.

Note: English-language books only

To order books online:
oreilly.com/store

For questions about products or an order:
orders@oreilly.com

To sign up to get topic-specific email announcements and/or news about upcoming books, conferences, special offers, and new technologies:
elists@oreilly.com

For technical questions about book content:
booktech@oreilly.com

To submit new book proposals to our editors:
proposals@oreilly.com

O'Reilly books are available in multiple DRM-free ebook formats. For more information:
oreilly.com/ebooks

O'REILLY®

Spreading the knowledge of innovators   oreilly.com

CPSIA information can be obtained
at www.ICGtesting.com
Printed in the USA
BVOW08s1027151217
502876BV00013B/212/P